TABLE OF CONTENTS

Page

ACRONYMS

BBC	British Broadcasting Corporation
CBS	Columbia Broadcasting System
CIA	Central Intelligence Agency
CIKR	Critical Infrastructure and Key Resources
CNN	Cable News Network
CSS	Central Security Service
DC3	Department of Defense Cyber Crime Center
DHS	Department of Homeland Security
DOD	Department of Defense
DoJ	Department of Justice
EO	Executive Order
FAA	Foreign Intelligence Surveillance Act (FISA) Amendments Act
FBI	Federal Bureau of Investigation
FEMA	Federal Emergency Management Agency
FISA	Foreign Intelligence Surveillance Act
FISC	Foreign Intelligence Surveillance Court
HSOC	Homeland Security Operations Center
HSPD	Homeland Security Presidential Directive
IC	Intelligence Community
IIMG	Interagency Incident Management Group
INTERPOL	International Criminal Police Organization
JCC	Joint Cyberspace Center
JCE	Joint Coordination Element

NBC	National Broadcasting Company
NCCIC	National Cybersecurity and Communications Integration Center
NCIJTF	National Cyber Joint Investigative Task Force
NCIRP	National Cyber Incident Response Plan
NCRCG	National Cyber Response Coordination Group
NCSC	National Cybersecurity Center
NCSD	National Cyber Security Division
NDS	National Defense Strategy
NICC	National Infrastructure Coordinating Center
NIMS	National Incident Management System
NMS	National Military Strategy
NOC	National Operations Center
NRF	National Response Framework
NRP	National Response Plan
NSA	National Security Agency
NSPD	National Security Presidential Directive
NSS	National Security Strategy
NTOC	National Security Agency/Central Security Service Threat Operations Center
PIN	Personal Identification Number
PPD	Presidential Policy Directive
PR/TT	Pen Register / Trap and Trace
SIGINT	Signal Intelligence
SQL	Structured Query Language
U.S.	United States

USC	United States Code
USCYBERCOM	United States Cyber Command
USNORTHCOM	United States Northern Command
USPACOM	United States Pacific Command
USSTRATCOM	United States Strategic Command

ILLUSTRATIONS

Page

TABLES

CHAPTER 1

INTRODUCTION

Cybersecurity threats represent one of the most serious national security, public safety, and economic challenges we face as a nation.
— President Barack Obama, *2010 National Security Strategy*

Research Question

This research examines the Department of Defense's role in homeland security as it relates to the defense of cyberspace necessary for the United States economy to function. The study views Department of Defense's role in concert with the role of the Department of Homeland Security as lead agent for homeland security. Both Departments of Defense and Homeland Security have roles in protecting the Internet where much of our financial information resides. Cyberspace activity blurs and crosses the lines between homeland security and homeland defense. Sovereign borders define national air, land and sea versus the ever-changing non-geography centered terrain of cyberspace. The transnational nature of the Internet creates a more ambiguous climate; cyberspace attacks do not occur solely within a nation's borders or solely outside of the sovereign territory. Instead, cyberspace allows criminals, terrorists, and even nation states to attack our economy from inside and outside our borders, simultaneously. Differentiating between criminal activities, terrorist actions, and acts of war is challenging. This study will focus on the applicable national strategy, policy, and laws that determine the roles and responsibilities of the two departments in homeland security of our economy as well as the public acceptance of both current and future efforts to secure cyberspace.

To focus this research, the primary research question is: What is the future role of the DOD in defending cyberspace supporting the electronic-commerce of the United States in homeland security? Secondary research questions are: Based on public response since Edward Snowden leaked information on National Security Agency collection programs on 5 June 2013 (Szoldra 2014), What is the public opinion to change or increase the roles or responsibilities of the Department of Defense to protect electronic commerce and the cyberspace that it relies on? What can the Department of Defense do better, or differently, to protect the United States electronic commerce from attacks on the sovereign cyberspace?

Background

In 2007, hackers breached the computer network of Heartland Payment Systems and remained within the system for months (Acohido 2009). Attackers compromised one-hundred-and-thirty-million debit and credit cards. Investigations reveled the source of the attacks and eventually traced the incident to four Russians, one Ukrainian, and Albert Gonzalez from the United States (Kitten 2013b).

In May 2009, President Barack Obama identified cyber-security "as one of the most serious economic and national security challenges we face as a nation" (U.S. President 2009a, 1). The anticipated looming attacks on the horizon were reasons to be cautious and suspicious. Throughout the years, even with policy changes, the attacks have continued to penetrate United States networks and the systems that contain some of our most sensitive data including key information to tap into our banking systems through debit and credit card information.

In July of 2009, both the United States and South Korea were the recipients of three waves of cyber-attacks. Among the victims of the third waves of attacks was the South Korea infrastructure, paralyzing Internet based banking (Sudworth 2009). A similar attack brought banking to a halt in South Korea in 2011 (BBC News 2011a) and again in 2013 with three different banks disrupted simultaneously (Sang-Hun 2013). In the attacks of 2009, 2011, and 2013, banking was disrupted or disabled. In all three of the incidents, North Korea is the suspect leading the attacks. The United States is fortunate that attackers have not affected us as severely as South Korea. However, that does not mean that the United States is invulnerable to an attack of this sort. Successful cyber-attacks continue showing that the United States is vulnerable in its own way.

The attacks have continued into the present day. In December 2013, the retail giant Target was the victim of one of the largest cyber-attacks in history. Hackers infiltrated the systems that were used to process and store information connected to every point of sale terminal in the United States Target infrastructure. Criminals stole the account information of up to seventy-million Americans in the form of stolen credit and debit card information, encrypted debit Personal Information Numbers, electronic-mail addresses, and other personal information (Target Brands Inc. 2014b). The malware exfiltrated information starting on 2 December 2013 and continued until Target intervened on 15 December 2013. The attacks aimed to gain the most amount of information during the Christmas holiday shopping season (Riley et al. 2014).

Hackers gained access through a maintenance company to uploaded malware onto the main computers of the Target chain. With access to Target's network, the hackers distributed the malware through Target's network to each of the point of sale terminals

3

connected to the main computer. On 30 November, Target's security operations center in Minneapolis, Minnesota failed to react to the situation. On 2 December, the malware began exfiltration of data to three staging computers in the United States. The attack forwarded information to computers in Ashburn Virginia, Provo Utah, and Los Angeles California then onward to Moscow, Russia (Riley et al. 2014). Target finally stopped the breach, but not before the compromise of seventy million account-credentials overseas (Target Brands Inc. 2014b). More than four years after President Obama identified cyber-security as one of America's most serious economic challenges, attacks were still placing our economy at risk.

The United States economy relies on the power of the American dollar and the trustworthiness of our electronic banking and finance systems. These systems rely on cyberspace to send financial information back and forth. However, the systems that maintain our credit card and debit card information are not secure and have been under consistent attack. With assaults continuing, and millions of American's financial information in jeopardy, the next attack could jeopardize the trustworthiness of the United States electronic banking system. American's rely on the electronic systems to store, retrieve, and transfer money and pay for goods and services. These systems rely on cyberspace to move the financial information from one point to another. Internet based infrastructure is used to pay for goods and services by either cashing a check immediately, conducting debit or credit card purchases, or receiving cash through Automated Teller Machines. The United States does not have the quantity of brick and mortar banks or credit unions to allow all transactions to convert to hard currency. The United States cannot convert back to an all cash economy without significant building of banks and credit unions. Any attempt to make this shift will require significant time and resources. Without the trust in cyberspace based financial transactions, the American economy could come to a screeching halt.

Presidents George W. Bush and Barack Obama both have instituted policies to protect cyberspace and spoken on the dangers of cyberspace intrusions. However, these policies have not stopped the cyber-attackers from stealing important financial and private information. Even if the United States does not have a good plan to respond to these threats, the Federal Government has an inherit right and responsibility to ensure our economy will continue to function. That responsibility mandates a Federal Government role in cyberspace security. Laws have codified many roles and responsibilities, but the attacks continue and our economy is not entirely safe.

Assumptions

Two key assumptions form the basis of this research study. The first questions the involvement of the Department of Defense. The second assumption is the acceptance of the American people.

The first assumption is that the Department of Defense can and should do something more to secure and defend the economic cyberspace of the United States. The Department of Defense has a significant cyberspace capability. However, the Department of Homeland Security has the mission to protect the security of the United States while the Department of Defense has the responsibility to defend the United States. The Department of Defense has to work with the Department of Homeland Security for any homeland security related incidents. Other federal departments and agencies, such as the Department of Justice, have roles and responsibilities as well. An assumption of this study is that the various roles and responsibilities can be deconflicted to allow the Department of Defense to act in the best interest of the nation, when and where needed.

A second assumption is that the American people will accept a different, or possibly increased, role of the Department of Defense. The public reaction to the National Security Agency programs has not always been positive. Privacy rights are of significant importance to American citizens and many see the National Security Agency efforts as counter to privacy concerns. Part of the consternation of the programs seems to be the secret nature of what the agency is doing. Some visibility on cyberspace security operations and procedures may be required to gain public acceptance. Regardless, any approach must balance the need for security with the need for privacy, and the applicability of search and seizure laws.

Definitions

A set of applicable definitions is included in the glossary portion of this study. However, the following terms are key to understanding the issues this research discusses:

Cyber-crime is "any illegal activity that uses a computer as its primary means of commission. The U.S. Department of Justice expands the definition of cyber-crime to include any illegal activity that uses a computer for the storage of evidence" (Rouse 2010b).

Cyberterrorism is "the intimidation of civilian enterprise through the use of high technology to bring about political, religious, or ideological aims, actions that result in disabling or deleting critical infrastructure data or information" (Tafoya 2011).

Cyber-warfare "is any virtual conflict initiated as a politically motivated attack on an enemy's computer and information systems. Waged via the Internet, these attacks disable financial and organizational systems by stealing or altering classified data to undermine networks, websites and services" (Janssen 2014).

A hacker is an individual "or small groups of people (who) can illegally disrupt or gain access to a network or computer system" (U.S. Department of the Air Force 2011, 13).

Homeland defense is the "protection of United States Sovereignty, territory, domestic population, and critical infrastructure against external threats and aggression or other threats as directed by the President" (Joint Chiefs of Staff 2013a, GL8-GL9).

Homeland security is the "concerted national effort to prevent terrorist attacks within the United States, reduce America's vulnerability to terrorism, major disasters, and other emergencies; and minimize the damage and recover from attacks, major disasters, and other emergencies that occur" (Joint Chiefs of Staff 2013a, GL9).

Scope

This research is limited to the federal response to cyberspace attacks and data exfiltrations that occur on non-bank, Internet based means. Specifically, the study examines the storage, retrieval, and movement of credit and debit card information to determine what role the Federal Government has in the case of a security breach. The study also examines the success or failure of specific case studies regarding the exploitation of security holes in the economic cyberspace of commercial organizations.

This study does not include any non-Internet infrastructure used by any American payment card system or the non-Internet based information systems that banks and credit unions may use in the course of their operations. Specifically excluded are any telephone networks, private networks, and internal administrative networks that organizations may use to complete transactions without interfacing with the financial data itself, unless that network responsible for a breach of payment card information. Research is limited to the storage, retrieval, and transfer of credit and debit card information through the Internet.

Limitations

Defense counter measures and offensive capabilities within cyberspace are sensitive topics within the Department of Defense and rely heavily on the intelligence community for information related to the defense of cyberspace. Due to the sensitive nature of these activities, much of the documentation as well as the process and procedures are classified. This study will consider and use only open source and unclassified information. This study uses some previously classified documents. In the case of these documents, only the unclassified, or redacted portion of the documents is included as part of the research.

Delimitations

The United States Air Force has focused efforts to develop the capability to fly, fight, and win in air, space, and cyberspace. However, cyberspace is beyond the scope of a single military service. The Army, Navy, Marines, and several Department of Defense agencies have cyberspace capabilities as well. In an attempt to remove bias, this study focuses on the capabilities of the Department of Defense as a whole, which will include all military services, Defense agencies, the National Security Agency, and Unified Commands.

Significance of the Study

The focus of this study is on the roles and responsibilities of the Department of Defense. It will focus on cyberspace strategy, policy, and the roles this department plays in the protection of the United States economy that runs on cyberspace. The study will attempt to examine the gaps between the roles and responsibilities of the Departments of Defense and Homeland Security specifically with incidents that involve elements within the borders of the United States and simultaneously outside the borders of the United States. Transnational criminals that cross sovereign borders pose challenges to any response. The coordination and cooperation required for a simultaneous homeland defense and homeland security incident poses unique difficulties to both departments.

CHAPTER 2

LITERATURE REVIEW

The entire phenomenon of cyber war is shrouded in such government secrecy that it makes the Cold War look like a time of openness and transparency. The biggest secret in the world about cyber war may be that at the very same time the U.S. prepares for offensive cyber war, it is continuing policies that make it impossible to defend the nation effectively from cyber-attack.
— Richard A. Clarke and Robert K. Knake, *Cyber War*

The literature review examines United States strategy, policy, law, and other related documents to understand the roles and responsibilities of the federal departments and agencies in the protection of cyberspace. Challenges remain with many of these documents, as most are either law enforcement concerns happening within the United States or defense situations designed to look outside our sovereign borders, but not both. Cyberspace crosses national boundaries and can be difficult to define due to the distributed architecture of the Internet.

The study begins with the United States national policies and strategies and moves into department level strategy, policy, and procedures from the Department of Defense and the Department of Homeland Security. Open source reporting will be used to provide the public view of strategy, policy, and procedures as well as gain awareness of third party views of roles and responsibilities of the Federal Government and its' departments.

One challenge to study a topic is the complexity of the various national level policies, strategies, and procedures that lay out differing roles and responsibilities among a large audience of departments and agencies. This study examines national level documents in the literature review to determine what responsibilities exist in Federal

Agencies, the portion of cyberspace that those roles cover, and how those roles and responsibilities may affect the protection of the United Stated economic networks, software, and systems.

National Strategy and Policy

Several Federal Government level documents define national policy for the protection of financial information contained in cyberspace. These presidential level documents demonstrate a continual and increasing importance of how financial and payment information is stored, transmitted, and retrieved. Through time, the strategies emphasized the increased importance of the economy to keep the United States functioning.

Comprehensive National Cybersecurity Initiative

President Obama approved this policy approved in May 2009 as a continuation of the effort begun by President Bush. This White House document outlines twelve initiatives to help protect United States cyberspace and places the Department of Homeland Security's National Cybersecurity Center as a key player in securing the federal government's cyberspace networks and system. The title suggests that this document outlines how the United States will protect the cyberspace for the entire nation. However, the document focuses on how to protect the federal enterprise rather than the commercial interests of the United States. It calls for cooperation between the federal departments and agencies to security the government portion of cyberspace (U.S. President 2009a, 1).

International Strategy for Cyberspace

President Obama signed the *International Strategy for Cyberspace: Prosperity,
Security, and Openness in a Networked World* in May 2011. The directive states that
cyber-security is an obligation while also specifying the principles of "free speech and
association, privacy, and the free flow of information" (U.S. President 2011a, i). The
policy calls for international cooperation with partnerships, stakeholder organizations,
and the private sector, to protect cyberspace, specifically the Internet, against threats that
transcend national borders (U.S. President 2011a, 4, 11-12). The Strategy adopts a
defense objective of dissuading and deterring attacks on United States networks (U.S.
President 2011a, 12-13). The *Strategy* sees law enforcement and military effort
depending on international partners to adapt to the changing threats in cyberspace (U.S.
President 2011a, 19-21).

National Security Strategy

The *National Security Strategy (2010)* approved by President Obama describes
the security of cyberspace as "one of the most serious national security, public safety, and
economic challenges we face as a nation" (U.S. President 2010, 27). The *Strategy*
recognizes that the United States will not be able to protect itself against all cyber-
attacks. It places an emphasis on strengthening security and resilience at home (U.S.
President 2010, 18). It lists cyber as a domain that the military must have the capability to
leverage as a use of force, if needed (U.S. President 2010, 22). However, the protection
of cyberspace infrastructure is not something the Federal Government can do on its own.
The lines between homeland security and homeland defense are blurred. To bridge this
gap, the strategy relies on integration between homeland security and homeland defense

capabilities and international partners with the private sector to secure cyberspace (U.S. President 2010, 10, 26-27).

National Strategy for Homeland Security

President Bush approved and signed the *National Strategy for Homeland Security* on 5 October 2007. Written by the Homeland Security Council, it describes the approach to secure the homeland by integrating the "capabilities of local, Tribal, State, and Federal Governments, as well as those of the private and non-profit sectors, in order to secure the land, maritime, air, space, and cyber domains" (Homeland Security Council 2007, 5). It describes a need for awareness of terrorist activity within the cyber domain and prevention of terrorist exploitation of both the financial and cyber systems, among others. However, it divides the task of homeland security among seventeen sectors of critical infrastructure and key resources and divides protection of cyber infrastructure as cooperative efforts between "Federal, State, and local governments, along with the private sector" (Homeland Security Council 2007, 27-28). An overarching approach to integrate these various players specifically to respond to cyberspace attacks that happen literally at the speed of light is noticeably lacking.

National Strategy to Secure Cyberspace

The *National Strategy to Secure Cyberspace* (February 2003), was written just after the Department of Homeland Security was signed into law, but before the new department had taken over its responsibilities. This strategy outlines three strategic objectives to secure cyberspace: "prevent cyber-attacks against America's critical infrastructure, reduce national vulnerability to cyber-attacks, and minimize damage and recovery time from cyber-attacks that do occur" (U.S. President 2003d, viii). It acknowledges the dependency of the United States economy and national security on information technology and especially the Internet. The *Strategy* is concerned with cyber-attacks causing "debilitating disruption to our nation's critical infrastructure, economy, or national security" (U.S. President 2003d, viii). "It is the policy of the United States to prevent or minimize disruptions to critical information infrastructures and thereby protect the people, the economy, the essential human and government services, and the national security of the United States" (U.S. President 2003d, 13).

A key point of this strategy is partnerships between the Federal Government and industry to secure cyberspace. This strategy assigned the Department of Homeland Security as the focal point for managing cyberspace incidents. However, it needs help from other federal departments to coordinate, and communicate actions (U.S. President 2003d, 16-17). Seven federal department are Lead Agency and responsible to assist the Department of Homeland Security. The Lead Agencies of the Departments of Homeland Security, Treasury, Health and Human Services, Energy, Agriculture, Defense, and the Environmental Protection Agency have specific sectors to protect. Pertinent to this study is the Department of Treasury's role as Lead Agency over the banking and finance sector (U.S. President 2003d, 16).

Strategy to Combat Transnational Organized Crime

President Obama signed the *Strategy to Combat Transnational Organized Crime* in July 2011. This *Strategy* identifies cyber-crime as a threat to the international finance system (U.S. President 2011c, 7) and lists the United States Secret Service as the responsible agency to investigate cyber-crimes "through its 31 Electronic Crimes Tasks

Forces" (U.S. President 2011a, 7). The Federal Bureau of Investigation has a different role in cyberspace with its National Cyber Investigative Joint Task Force which serves as a "domestic focal point for 18 federal departments or agencies to coordinate, integrate, and share information related to cyber threat investigations" (U.S. President 2011a, 8). Under the Department of Justice, the International Organized Crime Intelligence and Operations Center bridges intelligence collection efforts, law enforcement agencies, and federal prosecutors to combat transnational organized crime's broad range of activities (U.S. President 2011a, 19). Finally, the Secret Service's cyber intelligence goal is to prevent and mitigate attacks against financial infrastructures through information collection and sharing (U.S. President 2011a, 23).

Executive Order 12333: United States Intelligence Activities (as amended)

Executive Order 12333 *United States Intelligence Activities*, authorizes the National Security Agency to collect, retain, analyze, and disseminate foreign signals intelligence (SIGINT) information on "foreign persons that occur wholly outside of the United States" (National Security Agency 2013). The Order was originally signed by President George Bush, but has been amended by President Obama three times by Executive Orders 13284 in 2003, Executive Order 13355 in 2004, and Executive Order 13470 in 2008 (U.S. President 2008b). The goal of this Executive Order is to aid the National Security Council by providing information to make decisions that protect and defend the United States (U.S. President 1981). The National Security Agency uses this authority, along with the authorities granted by the Foreign Intelligence Surveillance Court, to conduct much of its activities. However, the National Security Agency gathered United States citizen's incidental information in the process (National Security Agency 2013).

15

National Security Presidential Directive 54/
Homeland Security Presidential Directive 23
Cybersecurity Policy

This policy contains a single strategy as a single document with two titles as enacted on 8 January 2008. The document begins several mutually supportive initiatives created to help secure cyberspace in the United States (U.S. President 2009a, 1). The policy reduces current cyberspace vulnerabilities by establishing a "front line of defense against today's immediate threats" (U.S. President 2009a, 1) through shared situational awareness to include all levels of government as well as private sector partners (U.S. President 2009a, 1). It also promotes enhancing criminal investigation and intelligence collection, processing and analysis to enable national cybersecurity efforts. The Obama Administration adopted these recommendations and included them in President Obama's *Comprehensive National Cybersecurity Initiative* (U.S. President 2008a).

Presidential Policy Directive-28 Signals Intelligence

President Obama signed Presidential Policy Directive 28 *Signals Intelligence* on 17 January 2014 to direct and clarify how signals intelligence information may be gathered, stored and processed. It also discusses treating people with "dignity and respect" regardless of nationality (U.S. President 2014). The directive sets forth principles for signals intelligence activities, bulk collection of signals intelligence activities, and the safeguarding of personal information that may be collected during the course of signals intelligence activities (U.S. President 2014). The Federal Bureau of Investigation has specific exceptions to this policy in accordance with on-going investigations. However, this directive applies to all agencies of the Federal Government.

Department of Defense Strategy

Starting with the *Quadrennial Defense Review* and the *National Defense Strategy*, the Department of Defense has instituted strategy, policy, and procedure to protect and defend cyberspace infrastructure and information. The following selected documents outline how the Department of Defense and the military expect to defend the nation and assist with homeland security.

Department of Defense Strategy for Operating in Cyberspace

The Department of Defense formalized the *Strategy for Operating in Cyberspace* in July 2011. This strategy discusses the strengths of America's use of cyberspace and the vulnerabilities the nation may experience due to disruption or exploitation. Mitigation of risks to the United States cyberspace requires the Department of Defense to collaborate with interagency and international partners, as well as commercial and industrial partners, to maintain United States prosperity and security (U.S. Department of Defense 2011, 1). Threats to the nation are more than military targets and include attacks by criminals, nation states, and terrorist organizations. A whole of government approach will improve United States cyber-security (U.S. Department of Defense 2011, 3-4, 8). This strategy recognizes cyberspace as an operational domain and will organize, train, and equip to dominate this domain along with air, land, maritime, and space (U.S. Department of Defense 2011, 5).

National Defense Strategy

The *National Defense Strategy* is included as chapter II of the 2014 *Quadrennial Defense Review* (U.S. Secretary of Defense 2014, 10-25). The Department of Defense

17

places emphasis on three pillars: protecting the homeland, building global security, and projecting power to win decisively (U.S. Secretary of Defense 2014, 12). As part of the protecting the homeland, high priority will continue to be placed on cyber defense capabilities. The Department of Defense will stand ready to protect the nation against operations that threaten United States interests, as directed by the President (U.S. Secretary of Defense 2014, 14). Interagency coordination will continue with the Department of Homeland Security to improve critical infrastructure cyber-security (U.S. Secretary of Defense 2014, 15).

National Military Strategy

The latest version of the National Security Strategy is the 2011 document, *The National Military Strategy 2011: Redefining America's Military Leadership.* This Strategy is a subordinate document to the *2010 National Security Strategy.* Admiral M. G. Mullen, then Chairman of the Joint Chiefs of Staff, instituted the Strategy on 8 February 2011. The Strategy recognizes that transnational criminal actors, terrorist organizations, as well as state-sponsored cyber attackers are all threats to the globally connected cyberspace domain (Chairman of the Joint Chiefs of Staff 2011, 3). Global access to cyberspace is a key aspect of national security. The military will remain focused on ensuring access to this global domain to continue the "exchange of people, ideas, goods, information, and capital that are critical to the global economy" (Chairman of the Joint Chiefs of Staff 2011, 9). To ensure this access, United States Cyber Command will collaborate with interagency, international, industry, and non-governmental entities to ensure combatant commands are able to operate across cyberspace. If necessary, the Command will provide options to safeguard access and hold cyber attackers accountable.

The Strategy states that congress and the President will need to grant new authorities to continue this mission (Chairman of the Joint Chiefs of Staff 2011, 10). However, the Strategy does not elaborate on what new authorities may be required.

National Military Strategy for Cyberspace Operations

As cited in this study, the *National Military Strategy for Cyberspace Operations,* dated December 2006, is a redacted and declassified document that was formerly classified Secret. Large portions of this document have been blocked-out leaving portions of the *Strategy* unavailable to the public. This *Strategy* explains that the Department of Defense has been assigned "three main roles: defense of the Nation, national incident response, and critical infrastructure protection" (Joint Chiefs of Staff 2006, 1-2), to included defense of the homeland. In pursuit of this goal, the Department of Defense will collaborate with the Departments of Justice and Homeland Security as well as other federal departments and agencies (Joint Chiefs of Staff 2006, 2). The document repeatedly stresses working with law enforcement.

Of note is the list of legal authorities that allow the Department of Defense to execute roles and responsibilities within cyberspace as shown in table 1. The federal law section of the Literature Review portion of this study describes more fully these legal authorities.

US Code	Table 1. Department of Defense Legal Authorities			
US Code	Title	Key Focus	Principal Organization	Role in Cyberspace
Title 6	*Domestic Security*	Homeland Security	Department of Homeland Security	Security of US Cyberspace
Title 10	*Armed Forces*	National Defense	Department of Defense	Secure US Interests by Conducting Military Operations in Cyberspace
Title 18	*Crimes and Criminal Procedure*	Law Enforcement	Department of Justice	Crime Prevention, Apprehension, and Prosecution of Cyberspace Criminals
Title 32	*National Guard*	First Line Defense of the United States	Army National Guard, Air National Guard	Support Defense of US Interests in Cyberspace Through Critical Infrastructure Protection, Domestic Consequence Management and Other Homeland Defense-Related Activities
Title 40	*Public Buildings, Property, and Works*	Chief Information Officer Roles and Responsibilities	All Federal Departments and Agencies	Establish and Enforce Standards for Acquisition and Security of Information Technologies
Title 50	*War and National Defense*	Foreign Intelligence and Counter-Intelligence Activities	Intelligence Community Agencies Aligned Under the Office of the Director of National Intelligence	Intelligence Gathering Through Cyberspace on Foreign Intentions, Operations, and Capabilities

Source: Department of Defense, *The National Military Strategy for Cyberspace Operations* (Washington, DC: Department of Defense, 2006), A-1.

Quadrennial Defense Review

Secretary of Defense Chuck Hagel signed *The Quadrennial Defense Review* on 4 March 2014. The *Review* discusses the fiscal climate that will restrict force size and determine the priorities in the coming years and builds on the priorities developed in the *2012 Defense Strategic Guidance*. Three pillars are emphasized areas of focus: protecting the homeland, building global security, and projecting power to win decisively (U.S. Secretary of Defense 2014, V). As part of the effort to rebalance the force, investment efforts will be placed on training and equipment our forces to expand our cyber capabilities to support Combatant Commanders as well as counter attacks against the United States (U.S. Secretary of Defense 2014, VII, X).

The *Review* also discusses the future threats seen today for the nation. As part of those threats, attacks on cyberspace will continue to challenge the United States security and economy. Attacks will originate from individuals, organizations and nation states with diverse goals (U.S. Secretary of Defense 2014, 7). The Department of Defense will continue to stand up Cyber Mission Forces through 2016 to include "National Mission Forces that counter cyber-attacks against the United States" (U.S. Secretary of Defense 2014, 32-33). The Department of Defense will continue to work with interagency and international partners to improve cyber defense capabilities and mitigate risks (U.S. Secretary of Defense 2014, 33).

Chapter II of the *Quadrennial Defense Review* is the *National Defense Strategy*. This document is a separate entry in the literature review.

Strategy for Homeland Defense and
Defense Support of Civil Authorities

Secretary of Defense Leon Panetta released the *Strategy for Homeland Defense and Defense Support of Civil Authorities* in February 2013. Threats to the United States cyberspace infrastructure are recognized vulnerabilities from organized crime, terrorists, and nation states (U.S. Secretary of Defense 2013, 5). The Department of Defense will continue to work with the Department of Homeland Security, Federal Bureau of Investigation, and other interagency partners to protect the nation from cyber threats, as directed by the President (U.S. Secretary of Defense 2013, 6). *The Strategy* does not show *Cyberspace* as a component contributing to the mission of defending the territory

21

from direct attack, even with a broad understanding of fitting with other federal agencies (U.S. Secretary of Defense 2013, 9). However, cyberspace is a vector that could cause a complex catastrophe of extraordinary casualties, damage to the environment, or the economy. During a complex catastrophe, the Department of Defense will respond as quickly as possible to assist civil authorities (U.S. Secretary of Defense 2013, 16-17).

Joint Publications

Joint Publication 3-12, Cyberspace Operations

This Joint Publication is mentioned in Joint Publication 3-27, *Homeland Defense,* 29 July 2013 (Joint Chiefs of Staff 2013a, II-3, II-8, II-13, III-15, III-16, III-23, E-6), and Joint Publication 3-28, *Defense Support of Civil Authorities*, 31 July 2013 (Joint Chiefs of Staff 2013b, IV-3 and IV-14). However, this document is not available publically on the Joint Electronic Library at the time of this study (U.S. Department of Defense 2014). Open source information is a requirement for documents to be included in the literature review. Due to the lack of a publically released source, Joint Publication 3-12, *Cyberspace Operations,* is not included in this study. It is likely this document is in review awaiting publication.

Joint Publication 3-27, Homeland Defense

Joint Publication 3-27, *Homeland Defense,* 29 July 2013, is the joint doctrine that explains how the Department of Defense will plan, coordinate, and control operations to "defeat external threats to, and aggression against, the homeland, or against other threats as directed by the President" (Joint Chiefs of Staff 2013a, xiv). As part of this effort, cyberspace offense and defense operations are included alongside military engagements, peace operations, and global strike (Joint Chiefs of Staff 2013a, ix - x). Cyberspace is recognized as a strategic threat to the homeland (Joint Chiefs of Staff 2013a, I-4) from terrorist (Joint Chiefs of Staff 2013a, I-5) as well as threats to critical infrastructure (Joint Chiefs of Staff 2013a, I-11).

Homeland security and homeland defense functions may overlap between federal agencies and the Department of Defense (Joint Chiefs of Staff 2013a, xi). The Department of Homeland Security, with its subordinate National Cyber Security Division, serves as the focal point for the security of cyberspace within the United States (Joint Chiefs of Staff 2013a, II-3). United States Pacific Command and United States Northern Command have responsibilities to coordinate with United Stated Cyber Command to protect public networks against cyberspace attacks. This coordination may extend to direct conversation with the National Cyber Security Division (Joint Chiefs of Staff 2013a, II-3).

Unified Commands

United States Strategic Command

The United States Strategic Command is a unified combatant command under the Department of Defense. Its mission is to "detect, deter, and prevent strategic attacks against the United States and our Allies" (U.S. Strategic Command, Public Affairs Office 2014). United States Strategic Command has six priorities of which three that apply to this study: "build enduring relationships with partner organizations to confront the broad range of global challenges," "build cyberspace capability and capacity," and "anticipate change and confront uncertainty with agility and innovation" (U.S. Strategic Command, Public Affairs Office 2014). To perform cyberspace related tasks, United States Strategic

Command stood up United States Cyber Command on 23 June 2009 (U.S. Cyber Command Public Affairs 2013).

United States Cyberspace Command

The United States Cyber Command is a sub-unified command under United States Strategic Command. It has three focus areas, two of which apply to this study: "providing support to combatant commanders for execution of their missions around the world, and strengthening our nation's ability to withstand and respond to cyber-attack" (U.S. Cyber Command Public Affairs 2013).

United States Cyber Command has begun plans to stand up Cyber National Mission Force teams designed to defend the Department of Defense and the nation, as a capability to achieve these focus areas. The teams will be operational in 2016 and will be responsible for "defending the nation's critical infrastructure and key resources" (Pellerin 2014). "These defend-the-nation teams are not defensive teams; these are offensive teams that the Defense Department would use to defend the nation if it were attacked in cyberspace" (Pellerin 2013).

National Security Agency

The National Security Agency has published its strategy in the *NSA/CSS Strategy* (National Security Agency 2010). This document covers both the National Security Agency and the Central Security Service. The Director of the National Security Agency is simultaneously the Chief of the CSS (Hatch 2003). As part of that strategy, "Goal 1— succeeding in Today's Operations" (National Security Agency 2010) is pertinent in this research. Part of that goal includes detecting "strategic threats to U.S. political, economic, or military interests" (National Security Agency 2010) and collecting intelligence that will "uncover, prevent, mitigate, or counter attempts to compromise information or information technology that is critical to national interests" (National Security Agency 2010).

Department of Homeland Security Policy

Congress established the Department of Homeland Security in 2002 by consolidating several different functions into a single department through *Public Law 107-296*. Included as part of this department are the National Cybersecurity and Communications Integration Center, Immigration and Customs Enforcement, and the United States Secret Service. Each of the departments has a role and/or responsibility in investigating or preventing cyber related financial crime and homeland defense.

Department of Homeland Security Strategic Plan

The *Department of Homeland Security Strategic Plan: Fiscal Years 2012-2016* lists one mission, with several sub-missions, as safeguarding and securing cyberspace. Specifically, this mission includes protecting privately owned critical infrastructure that supports the financial services industry, among others (U.S. Secretary of Homeland Security 2012, 12-14). This strategy recognizes the complex nature of cyber-attacks, as well as the nature of the organizations chartered to protect cyberspace. Countering these complex attacks "requires us to adopt traditional roles and responsibilities across the national security spectrum and craft solutions that leverage the capabilities both inside and outside of government.

Memorandum of Agreement Regarding Cybersecurity

On 24 and 27 September 2010, Secretary of Defense Robert Gates and Secretary of Homeland Security, Janet Napolitano signed the *Memorandum of Agreement Between The Department of Homeland Security and the Department of Defense Regarding Cybersecurity* to improve interdepartmental collaboration to improve protection of the United States. The document is designed to bridge the departments' missions of homeland security and homeland defense (Napolitano and Gates 2010, 1).

The Department of Homeland Security, as part of this agreement, will assign personnel to work within the National Security Agency and the United States Cyber Command to assist with coordination, collaboration, and planning cyberspace response capabilities (Napolitano and Gates 2010, 1-2). Specifically included is the Department of Homeland Security's appointment of a Cybersecurity Coordination Director who will serve as the Senior Department of Homeland Security Representative to United States Cyber Command and work within the National Security Agency. The *Memorandum* also dedicates Department of Homeland Security personnel to work within a Joint Coordination Element in the National Security Agency and personnel assigned to work within the National Security Agency/Central Security Service Threat Operations Center (Napolitano and Gates 2010, 1-2).

The Department of Defense, as part of this agreement, will lead the Joint Coordination Element and the Threat Operations Center and provide necessary equipment for Department of Homeland Security staff to carry out their roles and responsibilities. Joint operational planning includes National Security Agency, United States Cyber Command, and Department of Homeland Security personnel. United States

Cyber Command will locate a Cyber Support Element within the Department of Homeland Security's National Cybersecurity and Communications Integration Center to support Department of Homeland Security and synchronize operations (Napolitano and Gates 2010, 3-4).

National Cyber Incident Response Plan

No final version of the *National Cyber Incident Response Plan* is available as of this research. However, the Federal Emergency Management Agency used the Interim Version of September 2010 (U.S. Department of Homeland Security 2010b) as a source document for cyberspace readiness exercises (Federal Emergency Management Agency 2013a).

The *National Cyber Incident Response Plan* defines four National Cyber Risk Alert Levels of cyber incidents based on the level of response. Table 2 shows these levels.

The Department of Homeland Security's National Cybersecurity and Communications Integration Center, is a "twenty-four hour, seven day a week, integrated operations center, that builds and maintains federal level situational awareness through a common operating picture for cyberspace" (U.S. Department of Homeland Security 2010b, 3-4, 12). It includes "a continuously updated, comprehensive picture of cyber threats" (U.S. Department of Homeland Security 2010b, 3-4, 12). Information for the common operating picture comes from Federal Government agencies, the intelligence community, law enforcement agencies, and private sector companies (U.S. Department of Homeland Security 2010b, 4). The National Cybersecurity and Communications Integration Center coordinates the Federal Government response for significant cyber incidents including National Cyber Risk Alert level two and higher events, as described

in table 2.

Table 2. National Cyber Risk Alert Levels			
Level	Label	Description of Risk	Level of Response
1	Severe	Highly disruptive levels of consequences are occurring or imminent	Response functions are overwhelmed, and top-level national executive authorities and engagements are essential. Exercise of mutual aid agreements and Federal/non-Federal assistance is essential.
2	Substantial	Observed or imminent degradation of critical functions with a moderate to significant level of consequences, possibly coupled with indicators of higher levels of consequences impending	Surged posture becomes indefinitely necessary, rather than only temporarily. The Department of Homeland Security (DHS) Secretary is engaged, and appropriate designation of authorities and activation of Federal capabilities such as the Cyber UCG take place. Other similar non-Federal incident response mechanisms are engaged.
3	Elevated	Early indications of, or the potential for but no indicators of, moderate to severe levels of consequences	Upward shift in precautionary measures occurs. Responding entities are capable of managing incidents/events within the parameters of normal, or slightly enhanced, operational posture.
4	Guarded	Baseline of risk acceptance	Baseline operations, regular information sharing, exercise of processes and procedures, reporting, and mitigation strategy continue without undue disruption or resource allocation.

Source: Department of Homeland Security, *National Cyber Incident Response Plan: Interim Version, September 2010* (Washington, DC: Department of Homeland Security, 2010), 3.

The Federal Cyber Incident Lanes describe the roles and responsibilities of the

Department of Homeland Security, intelligence community, Department of Defense, and

law enforcement agencies as shown in Appendix A of this study.

Four different coordination centers are responsible for organizing actions for

cyber incidents. The National Cybersecurity and Communications Integration Center is

the coordinating center for the Department of Homeland Security. The National Security

Agency/Central Security Service Threat Operations Center bridges information between the intelligence community and the Department of Defense. The United States Cyber Command's coordination center organizes efforts for the Department of Defense. Finally, the National Cyber Joint Investigative Task Force coordinates activities for law enforcement. Other interagency centers provide information to each of these centers in an attempt to synchronize actions (U.S. Department of Homeland Security 2010b, 9).

Due to the complexity of cyberspace incidents, the Department of Homeland Security may be in a supported or supporting relationship with other federal agencies. These relationships will depend on the threat (U.S. Department of Homeland Security 2010b, 9-11).

Appendixes to the *National Cyber Incident Response Plan* address the specific responsibilities of the Departments of Homeland Security, Defense, Justice, State, the intelligence community, other government agencies, and private sector organizations (U.S. Department of Homeland Security 2010b).

In respect to this study, Annex C of the *National Cyber Incident Response Plan* describes how the Department of Defense will integrate with interagency partners through a Cyber Unified Coordination Group Senior Official. Appendix A of this study, includes the full table that discusses these roles and responsibilities. Annex C does not mention how United States Cyber Command, its predecessor Joint Task Force-Global Network Operations, the National Security Agency/Central Security Service Threat Operations Center, or the Department of Defense Cyber Crime Center will integrate into any cyber incident response (U.S. Department of Homeland Security 2010b, C-1 - C-2).

National Response Plan

The *National Response Plan* is a "comprehensive approach to domestic incident management to prevent, prepare for, respond to, and recover from terrorist attacks, major disasters, and other emergencies" (U.S. Department of Homeland Security 2006, 1). The *National Response Framework* superseded the *National Response Plan* in January 2008 (U.S. Department of Homeland Security 2008a).

National Response Framework

The *National Response Framework* is a Department of Homeland Security document managed by the Federal Emergency Management Agency. It aims to connect federal, state, and local governments, as well as civilian organizations and citizens, to protect or recover from disaster of any type "regardless of scale, scope, and complexity" (U.S. Department of Homeland Security 2013a, 1). The *National Response Framework* outlines principles designed to promote partnerships, unity of effort, and readiness to respond to crisis. The document outlines that the Department of Defense, under the control of the Secretary of Defense, and National Guard Forces, under the command of the governor, may be asked to respond to a crisis to "save lives, protect property, and mitigate human suffering under imminently serious conditions" (U.S. Department of Homeland Security 2013a, 19). Under the authorities of the Stafford Act, governors may request Federal Government capabilities that are beyond those possessed by the state. Although there are no specific outlines for cyber incidents, the National Response Framework is broad enough that an attack on cyber infrastructure or information could potentially be included as an essential part of one of the Emergency Support Functions related to the economy or critical infrastructure (U.S. Department of Homeland Security 2013a, 32-34).

National Response Framework: Cyber Incident Annex

The Department of Homeland Security published the *National Response Framework: Cyber Incident Annex* in December 2004 as part of the *National Response Plan*. The Cyber Incident Annex is now part of the *National Response Framework* as Annex A. The Department of Homeland Security has not updated this *Annex* since 2004. The *Annex* prescribes policies, organizations, roles, and responsibilities to coordinate federal response to cyber incidents (U.S. Department of Homeland Security 2004a).

When a cyberspace incident occurs, the Secretary of Homeland Security may activate the Interagency Incident Management Group. The Interagency Incident Management Group will receive subject matter expertise and advice from the National Cyber Response Coordination Group (U.S. Department of Homeland Security 2004b, CYB-2). The National Cyber Response Coordination Group is an interagency organization comprised of members from federal agencies that have investigative and response roles to cyberspace incidents. During incidents of national importance, the National Cyber Response Coordination Group will coordinate with the Homeland Security Operations Center to share information with government and non-government responders (U.S. Department of Homeland Security 2004b, CYB-3).

A section of the Annex discusses the role of the Department of Defense. However, this portion of the Annex is out of date as it pre-dates the creation of United States Cyber Command. With the creation of the unified command, United States Cyber Command has the responsibilities of the former organization of Joint Task Force-Global

Network Operations as dictated in the Annex. With this mission, United States Cyber Command is responsible to respond to cyber-attacks and coordinate with both the Department of Homeland Security as well as law enforcement (U.S. Department of Homeland Security 2004b, CYB-3).

United States Secret Service

Secret Service Strategic Plan

The *Secret Service Strategic Plan* contains the goals, objectives, and strategies of the service. One of the objectives listed in the *Strategic Plan* is to "protect the nation's financial infrastructure through investigative activities" (U.S. Secret Service 2014b, 9). As part of this goal, "protecting financial infrastructure" and expanding the "ability to respond to cyber intrusions" are included (U.S. Secret Service 2014b, 9). Investigations are the core service that the Secret Service offers. The *Strategic Plan* does not mention proactive approaches to protect the financial infrastructure or the information the infrastructure contains.

Secret Service Annual Report

The *Secret Service Annual Report* captures the activity of the service in the preceding year. The 2013 report outlines cyber operations to protect the financial infrastructure. The focus is partner efforts to improve the investigative capabilities of both the Secret Service and other law enforcement agencies as well as collaboration activities through forty-five Financial Crimes Task Forces (U.S. Secret Service 2013, 23). In concert with academia, the private sector, and various law enforcement agencies, thirty-three Electronic Crimes Task Forces, "successfully prevent cyber-attacks before they occur" (U.S. Secret Service 2013, 23). This seems to indicate a proactive approach by the Secret Service. However, the *Annual Report* does not provide details of the proactive approaches, or their employment. These unspecified programs have produced some success. In Fiscal Year "2013, the Secret Service prevented over $1.1 billion in fraud loss and identified more than $235 million in actual fraud loss in cyber-crime investigations" (U.S. Secret Service 2013, 23).

Department of Justice

The Department of Justice is a law enforcement entity designed to enforce the legal code of the United States. As part of that mission, the Federal Bureau of Investigation is a big component. The Department focuses on enforcement of laws after a crime has been committed. Proactive approaches are not the focus, but are considered.

Department of Justice Strategic Plan

The *Department of Justice Fiscal Years 2014-2018 Strategic Plan* sets strategic goals, priority goals, and objectives. Two specific objectives relate to this study to address cyberspace attacks: cyber-crime and cyberterrorism.

The first objective is to "combat cyber-based threats and attacks through the use of all available tools, strong public-private partnerships, and the investigation and prosecution of cyber threat actors" (The Attorney General 2013, 13-14). Cyber activities that are both terrorist actions and attack the economy are components addressed by this objective. To meet this goal, the Department of Justice will use an "all-tools approach" that includes "civil enforcement, regulatory enforcement, supply chain efforts, or other operations" (The Attorney General 2013, 19). Routine collaboration with other federal and law enforcement agencies, including cooperation with the International Criminal Police Organization (INTERPOL), is adopted as routine activity to combat cyber-crime and terrorism (The Attorney General 2013, 19).

The second related objective is to "investigate and prosecute corruption, economic crimes, and transnational organized crime" (The Attorney General 2013, 30-34). The Department of Justice recognizes that bank fraud utilizing the Internet poses "very severe threats to the United States' economy" (The Attorney General 2013, 30). To meet this objective, the Department of Justice will work with other federal departments, domestic, and international law enforcement agencies to unify a broad law enforcement effort (The Attorney General 2013, 31-34; Department of the Air Force 2012).

Federal Bureau of Investigation

The Federal Bureau of Investigation's priorities are contained within the Bureau's strategy document, *Today's FBI Facts and Figures 2013-2014*. One of the priorities of the Federal Bureau of Investigation that relates to this study is to "protect the United States against cyber-based attacks and high-technology crimes" (Federal Bureau of Investigation 2014c, 7). To meet this protection mission, the Bureau is collaborating with all levels of federal and state government agencies including the intelligence community (Federal Bureau of Investigation 2014c, 25). Within the Bureau's own intelligence functions, cyber fusion cells collect information to drive operations to protect the nation from foreign intelligence operations, terrorists, and criminal actors (Federal Bureau of Investigation 2014c, 30, 36). "The [Federal Bureau of Investigation] is the lead federal agency for investigating cyber-attacks by criminals, overseas adversaries, and terrorists" (Federal Bureau of Investigation 2014c, 36). As part of this effort, the Bureau leads the

National Cyber Investigative Joint Task Force that addresses cyber threats by bringing together eighteen agencies including law enforcement, military, and intelligence (Federal Bureau of Investigation 2014c, 55). Investigation of crimes after the fact is the focus of this document rather than proactive approaches to avoid or mitigate incidents.

Federal Laws and Legislation

The following selected federal laws and legislation outline the roles and responsibilities of government agencies. They also define authorities and prohibitions that government agencies must follow. Many of these laws have the intent of protecting the constitutional rights of the citizens of the United States and limit the actions that the government may take. Many of these laws display the idea of an open and free society that the United States' citizens hold in high regard.

Stafford Disaster Relief and Emergency Assistance Act

The *Stafford Disaster Relief and Emergency Assistance Act (Stafford Act)* gives the states the means to request federal emergency assistance. The act predominantly aims at natural disasters. However, it does include manmade disasters as well. Section 502 states that in any emergency the President may

> direct any Federal agency, with or without reimbursement, to utilize its authorities and resources grated to it under Federal law (including personnel, equipment, supplies, facilities, and managerial, technical and advisory services) in support of State and local emergency assistance efforts to save lives, property and public health and safety, and lessor or avert the threat of a catastrophe, including precautionary evacuations. (Federal Emergency Management Agency 2013b, Sec 502)

Although not specified, this law has the potential for the President to authorize the Department of Defense to leverage cyberspace technical expertise to assist states with a cyberspace related disaster.

United States Code, Title 6–Domestic Security

Title 6–*Domestic Security* outlines the roles and responsibilities of the Department of Homeland Security (U.S. Government 2013a). Of special note is the lack of a specific definition for either domestic security or homeland security.

Related to this study, 6 USC § 121 covers interdepartmental coordination efforts. Under section 121, the Department of Homeland Security and Department of Defense are required to collaborate to share cyberspace security information to improve efficiencies, build on technical expertise, and synchronize efforts for planning, and ongoing operations (U.S. Government 2013a, 21).

Upon request, 6 USC § 143 allows private entities to request assistance to improve their cybersecurity of critical information systems. Related to this effort is Section 144, which requires the Department of Homeland Security to set up local teams of experts to help communities respond and recover from breaches to their information infrastructure (U.S. Government 2013a, 48).

United States Code, Title 10–Armed Forces

United States Code Title 10 "contains the organic law governing the Armed Forces of the United States and provides for the organization of the Department of Defense, including the military departments, and the reserve components, and the organization, training, and equipping of forces" (U.S. Department of the Air Force 2012, 84).

Related to this study, 10 USC § 111 specifically addresses military activities in cyberspace. The law provides that "the Department of Defense has the capability, and upon direction by the President may conduct offensive operations in cyberspace to defend our Nation, Allies, and interests" (U.S. Government 2013b, 27).

10 USC § 113 also directs the Secretary of Defense to develop contingency plans to respond to several scenarios including nuclear detonation, biological attack, and cyber-attack. The scenarios developed must include two versions: one with National Guard forces only and a second with both National Guard and active duty forces (U.S. Government 2013b, 45).

10 USC § 2224 provides for the United States Cyber Command and delineates the authorities, capabilities, and oversight of peacetime and wartime missions (U.S. Government 2013b, 1208).

United States Code, Title 18 – Crimes and Criminal Procedure

United States Code Title 18 "provides the criminal penal code and procedure for the Federal Government and is applicable to . . . law enforcement activities" (U.S. Department of the Air Force 2012, 84).

Under 18 USC § 175, the Attorney General may request the Secretary of Defense to assist with law enforcement activities involving biological weapons (U.S. Government 2013c, 42-45). Similarly, 18 USC § 229E authorize similar support involving chemical weapons (U.S. Government 2013c, 82-82), § 831 with explosive and other dangerous articles (United States Government 2013c, 179-180), and § 2332 with terrorism and weapons of mass destruction (U.S. Government 2013c, 542-549). Assistance may include arrests, searches, and seizures or other activities incidental to law enforcement.

18 USC § 2314 addresses the transportation of stolen goods, counterfeiting, and money. This portion of the law applies to cyberspace as well, if the value of the theft is $5,000 or more (U.S. Government 2013c, 526-528). 18 USC § 2318 further builds on this idea by addressing intellectual property rights of copyright holders, including computer programs (U.S. Government 2013c, 529-532). Since many malware mask and hide in an attempt to look like another program, this section is a legal foundation against cyber-attackers using some types of software.

In *The National Military Strategy for Cyberspace*, the Department of Defense has summarized its cyberspace related Title 18 roles and responsibilities as "crime prevention, apprehension, and prosecution of cyberspace criminals" (Joint Chiefs of Staff 2006, A-1).

United States Code, Title 32–National Guard

United States Code Title 32 "is a compilation of federal laws pertaining to the militia, the Army National Guard of the United States, and the Air National Guard of the United States" (U.S. Department of the Air Force 2012, 84).

Under 32 USC § 102, the Army National Guard and the Air National Guard are codified as part of the first line of defense for the United States and its territories (U.S. Government 2012, 4). Unless federalized, the state or territorial Governor retains jurisdiction over the assigned National Guard forces. With the approval of the Governor, the National Guard may perform law enforcement duties of that state or territory (U.S. Government 2012, 11-13).

Under 32 USC chapter 9, National Guard military forces may perform homeland defense activities under the jurisdiction of the Secretary of Defense (Title 32-National Guard 2012, 52).

The Department of Defense has clarified its cyberspace related Title 32 roles and responsibilities as "support defense of U.S. interests in cyberspace through critical infrastructure protection, domestic consequence management and other homeland defense-related activities" (Joint Chiefs of Staff 2006, A-1).

United States Code, Title 50 – War and National Defense

United States Code Title 50 "includes authorities related to foreign intelligence surveillance" (U.S. Department of the Air Force 2012, 84). In relation to this study, chapter 36 and chapter 47 are directly relevant (U.S. Government 2011).

Chapter 36, subchapter I, covers electronic surveillance. This subchapter restricts the collection of information from United States citizens (U.S. Government 2014b). Specifically allowed is communication with law enforcement organizations to protect against actual or potential attacks from a foreign power (U.S. Government 2014c).

Chapter 47 of this code is the "National Security Agency Act of 1959" (U.S. Government 2014d). This law establishes the National Security Agency as an organization assigned to the Department of Defense and authorizes the Director of the National Security Agency to expend money for specific purposes to lead the Agency (U.S. Government 1959).

Foreign Intelligence Surveillance Act

The *Foreign Intelligence Surveillance Act of 1978* (FISA) was originally published on 25 October 1978 as Public Law 95-511, or 50 USC § 1801 (U.S. Government 1978). "FISA provides . . . the exclusive means for intercepting the content of communications in the United States for foreign intelligence purposes" (Goldsmith 2004, 19).

This law allows for collection of information on activities sponsored or controlled by foreign powers, or their agents, within the United States as approved by the Foreign Intelligence Surveillance Court (Goldsmith 2004, 19-20). It also allows for collection regarding terrorist organizations or activities (U.S. Government 1978). However, the *Foreign Intelligence Surveillance Act* does not allow for collection on criminal activities. The definition of a foreign power, as listed in the statute, requires a foreign government, international terrorist organization, or foreign political organization to be in control of information or an activity. A request to collect information in the United States must meet this definition. The *Foreign Intelligence Surveillance Act* does not authorize intelligence collection for other activity, such as transnational crime (U.S. Government 1978).

Protect America Act of 2007 (Patriot Act)

The *Protect America Act of 2007* is an amendment of the *Foreign Intelligence Surveillance Act* (U.S. Department of Justice 2007). The *Patriot Act*, as it is better known, became law on 5 August 2007 (U.S. Department of Justice 2014). This law grants additional rights to law enforcement by adapting to the ever-changing technological environment and streamlines the judicial process to request warrants (U.S. Department of Justice 2014).

The global nature of terrorism made many of the former criminal surveillance laws obsolete. Terrorists plan an activity in one part of the country and execute it in an entire different part of the country. Prior to the *Patriot Act*, the law required warrants filed in the district court where the terrorist act was expected or committed. This law streamlines the warrant process and allows any district to approve a warrant for surveillance, greatly aiding law enforcement efforts to stop terrorist organizations (U.S. Department of Justice 2014).

Under this law, hackers are treated the same as intruders and allows victims to request and receive law enforcement assistance by defining electronic trespassing to be similar to physical trespassing (U.S. Department of Justice 2014).

The law also promotes cooperation between law enforcement agencies, the intelligence community, and the Department of Defense by removing barriers to information sharing and allowing coordination to improve national security. Interagency cooperation improves information to be gathered from various agencies to better "connect the dots" (U.S. Department of Justice 2014) of terrorist activities.

United States v. Microsoft

Microsoft received a warrant regarding data was stored in its Microsoft Network (MSN) electronic mail system to provide information to a United States law enforcement agency for a narcotics case (Boehning and Toal 2014). The search warrant, issued on 4 December 2013, demanded information from Microsoft that was "stored at premises, owned, maintained, controlled, or operated by Microsoft Corporation" (Francis IV 2014).

Microsoft considered the warrant invalid as the information requested did not reside in a server located in the United States, but in Dublin, Ireland. Due to the geography of the data storage, Microsoft challenged the warrant in federal court (Ax 2014). On 25 April 2014, Judge James C. Francis ruled that Microsoft was required to turn over the information to law enforcement in the United States declaring, "Congress intended the [*Stored Communications Act*] for [Internet Service Providers] to produce information under their control, albeit stored abroad" (Van Voris 2014). Microsoft appealed the ruling. On 31 July 2014, United States District Court Judge Loretta Preska upheld the original decision. However, she delayed enforcing the ruling pending appeal by Microsoft. Continued legal action is expected (Boehning and Toal 2014).

Third Party Opinion

Many technical news writers have wrote on the security breakdowns surrounding the Target data breach in December 2013, as well as the course of action that Target and others took to help safeguard the systems both during and after the events. Writers have also captured opinions and reactions to the acceptance or rejection of the National Security Agencies' tools to monitor cyberspace activity.

In addition to journalists, privacy advocacy groups have written public opinion pieces on what the Federal Government is doing in regards to monitoring activity in cyberspace. There is no one overarching opinion on what the government should or should not do. However, many individuals and organizations are vocal about privacy rights and security requirements. Large portions of these opinions are the result of documents that Edward Snowden released showing what the National Security Agency is doing.

Some of the Snowden information, although freely available on the Internet, may remain classified. In an effort to avoid any further transmission of classified information, explanations, and the citations that follow, are limited. The importance of Snowden's revelations to this study is acceptance or rejection of surveillance programs from both public and private sectors and not the programs Snowden disclosed.

Privacy Rights, Advocacy, and the
Edward Snowden Revelations

In March 2012, Snowden worked for Dell Corporation as a contract employee working within a National Security Agency facility in Hawaii. A year later, he accepted a job as a contract employee of Booz Allen Hamilton, also working for the National Security Agency. During these jobs, Snowden received access to highly classified information (Cole and Brunker 2014). Beginning in May of that same year, he began distributing documents to media including The Washington Post and The Guardian (Cole and Brunker 2014). On 6 June 2013, the first article related to the classified documents surfaced through the media (U.S. Defense Intelligence Agency, 2013). The resulting documents spurred concern from both private and public sectors. Privacy advocate groups, members of the United States Congress, and the international community have voiced concerns about the National Security Agency's surveillance programs. The press has reported the disclosure widely with domestic and international reports (CNN 2014).

Declassification of Snowden Related Documents and Programs

In response to the Snowden revelations, President Obama released Presidential Policy Directive-28: *Signals Intelligence Activities,* on 17 January 2014. This document outlined refinements to the Intelligence Community including limitations on bulk collection, and protection of personal information (U.S. President 2014, 3-5). The *Policy* also directed Federal Agencies to declassify as much as practical. Based on that guidance, several National Security Agency capabilities were declassified.

The Office of the Director of National Intelligence released several declassified and redacted documents on 22 May 2014. Included in the document release were statements by former Director of National Intelligence, John D. Negroponte on the existence of telephone monitoring activities by the National Security Agency to investigate, track, and locate terrorists and their activities (U.S. District Court Northern District in California, 2006).

The Office of the Director of National Intelligence also released a redacted and declassified report on the Snowden information leak. The *Information Review Task Force-2 Initial Assessment: Impacts Resulting from the Compromise of Classified Material by a Former NSA Contractor* confirms that information was exposed that was contained in intelligence computer systems (U.S. Defense Intelligence Agency, 2013). However, the report did not validate any programs or capabilities disclosed by Snowden.

On 11 August 2014, additional information was released that confirmed the National Security Agency's collection of electronic-mail metadata such as the "to, from and cc lines of emails" (U.S. Office of the Director of National Intelligence, 2014). These Internet communications collections were under the auspices of Section 402 of the Foreign Intelligence Surveillance Act (U.S. Office of the Director of National Intelligence, 2014).

Privacy Rights and Civil Liberties Organizations Response

Numerous Privacy Rights and Civil Liberties Organizations have voiced concerns about the constitutionality and legal standing regarding the *Patriot Act* and surveillance by both the Federal Bureau of Investigation and the National Security Agency on persons within the United States. The following is not an all-inclusive list of those organizations, but a representative sampling of the opinion presented to and by the American people.

An 8 September 2013 article by the American Civil Liberties Union, described a dishonest United States Government that is impeding on the privacy rights of American citizens on a regular basis. The article describes the National Security Agency's programs that gather information under a wide umbrella of foreign collection. These programs monitor Americans as part of that collection effort. One of the largest concerns is that warrants are not required to search collected and stored information (Kaufman 2013).

The American Civil Liberties Union filed a complaint in the United States District Court, Southern District of New York, on 11 June 2013. The lawsuit challenged the constitutionality of the "dragnet acquisition of Plaintiffs' telephone records under Section 215 of the *Patriot Act*" (American Civil Liberties Union 2013). Supporters filed amicus briefs on 26 August, 30 August, and 4 September. On 27 December 2013, United States District Judge William H. Pauley III ruled in the case that the National Security Agency's bulk collection of telephone metadata was lawful and dismissed the American Civil Liberty Union's case. However, the case continues with an appeal filed by the plaintiffs on 6 March 2014 with seven amicus briefs filed on 13 March 2014 supporting the appeal (American Civil Liberties Union 2014).

The Brennan Center for Justice at the New York University School of Law has actively voiced concern for the National Security Agency surveillance programs. Reports were compiled in 2011 (Berman 2011) and again on 28 August 2014. The reports documented the Center's concerns about the surveillance by both the Federal Bureau of Investigation and the National Security Agency. Forty-three privacy advocates and organizations from both liberal and conservative political affiliations signed the report. Leaders of the Senate and the House of Representatives, and the Federal Government's Privacy and Civil Liberties Oversight Board, received both reports. The reports achieved some of their goals. On 23 January 2014, the Center reported that the Privacy Board called for an end to the National Security Agency's bulk collection program and that President Obama announced reforms to National Security Agency surveillance (Brennan Center for Justice 2014).

On 17 January 2006, the Center for Constitutional Rights filed a lawsuit to challenge the National Security Agency's monitoring of people located within the United States (Center for Constitutional Rights 2014). The lawsuit challenged the constitutionality of the National Security Agency surveillance within the United States of telephone calls and electronic mail (Center for Constitutional Rights 2013). On 10 June 2013, the Ninth Circuit Court of Appeals dismissed the lawsuit against President Obama and the Director of the National Security Agency, but the reasoning was not agreeable to the plaintiffs (Center for Constitutional Rights 2013).

The Privacy Advisor, in a 12 June 2013 article, reported that more than 80 privacy advocate organizations contacted Congress asking for their support to force the National Security Agency to stop it's "dragnet surveillance" (Barcy 2013). Both liberal and conservative groups voiced concerns of constitutional violations against the First Amendment freedom of speech and the Fourth Amendment prohibition of unreasonable searches and seizures (The National Archives 2014).

<u>News Media Reports</u>

Several major news services reported on the Snowden revelations and the response by individuals, political leaders, judicial districts, and privacy advocates. The following articles are not an all-inclusive list of all news organizations, but a representative sampling of the news reported as related to the exposure of National Security Agency programs.

The Washington Post produced several news articles regarding Snowden and the National Security Agency surveillance activities. Laura Donohue challenges the legal standing of the National Security Agency's surveillance programs and charges that the Foreign Intelligence Surveillance Court may not be doing its job to protect Fourth Amendment rights of United States citizens (Donohue 2013). Another article by Barton Gellman, discusses an internal National Security audit that identified 2,776 violations of the Foreign Intelligence Surveillance Court rules (Gellman 2013). The violations of the Fourth Amendment of the *Constitution* and mistakes by the National Security Agency have received notable reporting by The Washington Post. The book *NSA Secrets: Government Spying in the Internet Age* captures many of these *Washington Post* articles (The Washington Post 2013).

Cable News Network (CNN) also had extensive reporting on the Snowden leaks and public reaction to the surveillance activities. On 16 December 2013, Cable News Network reported on United States District Judge Richard Leon's preliminary ruling regarding National Security Agency's bulk collection of metadata. Judge Leon believes the bulk collection of information on American citizens is a violation of the Fourth Amendment of the *Constitution*. However, he put off enforcement of his decision pending a government appeal (Mears and Perez 2013). In another article, Arjun Sethi reported on the privacy concerns of Americans caught up in the National Security Agency's surveillance operations. The information disclosed by Snowden revealed the extent of data collection on United States citizens and has encouraged Congress to act. The House of Representatives is working to limit the surveillance powers of the intelligence community by passing the *USA Freedom Act* in May 2014 (Sethi 2014). The *Act* is currently awaiting action by the Senate.

Industry Reaction to Surveillance

Several corporations revealed involvement in providing information to the National Security Agency. The following is a representative sampling of the statements of industry as revealed by Yahoo, Verizon, and Microsoft. These reports are not an all-inclusive list of all corporations connected with the National Security Agency surveillance revelations.

Digital Trends reported in its 12 September 2014 article, "Yahoo says it faced $250,000-a-day fine for opposing NSA data" demand, that the United States Government threatened the online service with a substantial fine if it did not turn over user information. Yahoo fought back and took their grievance to the Foreign Intelligence Surveillance Court in 2007, but the court upheld the government order. According to Rob Bell, representing Yahoo's legal team, Yahoo is committed to the protection of online data (Mogg 2014). This example of Yahoo's involvement with government surveillance demonstrates that some corporations are willing to stand up for the privacy rights of the online community.

The Associated Press reported on 20 December 2013 about Verizon's plans to disclose its involvement with the National Security Agency. In the article, "Verizon plans transparency report on phone record requests, working with NSA," Verizon announced its plans to report semi-annually on the law enforcement requests for information that Verizon has received in an effort to provide transparency (Associated Press 2013). Related to those disclosures, the Foreign Intelligence Surveillance Court declassified a report in September 2013 that stated that no company has challenged a directive to turn over bulk phone records (Associated Press 2013).

On 6 June 2013, Microsoft released a statement regarding its involvement in National Security Agency's surveillance efforts. The statement read, in part, "we provide customer data only when we receive a legally binding order or subpoena to do so, and never on a voluntary basis. In addition we only ever comply with orders for requests about specific accounts or identifiers" (Microsoft Corporation 2013).

Seny Kamara, a member of Microsoft Research, proposed a software fix in April 2014 that would alleviate some of the privacy issues with the National Security Agency's surveillance programs (Kamara 2014b). His proposal would restructure the National Security Agency's databases through a program called *MetaCrypt*. The program would allow information to be stored encrypted and unavailable for direct access while still allowing for specific searches for authorized targets (Kamara 2014a). The *MetaCrypt* presentation posted on the Microsoft Research site is incomplete as the briefing notes are not available. However, the information in the slide show appears to be a promising software project that can better maintain privacy rights while still allowing the National Security Agency to perform its surveillance mission.

Government Response

Not all government responses have supported the National Security Agency. Utah and California lawmakers both independently introduced bills designed to cripple a National Security Agency data center under construction in Utah by denying electricity and water to the controversial facility. The data center will store the five-zettabytes of storage, or the equivalent of one-billion five-terabyte hard drives (Brandon 2013). The National Security Agency has not confirmed any specifics about the 1.5 million square foot, $1.7 billion facility (Associated Press 2014b). However, the facility uses sixty-five megawatts of power, according the Army Corp of Engineers (Brandon 2013). It also expects to use more than one-million gallons of water daily to cool the computer systems (Associated Press 2014b).

Republican Utah State Representative Marc Roberts proposed a bill that would greatly limit the activities at the data center by cutting off the water supply to the facility (Associated Press 2014b) in an effort to protect Forth Amendment rights of Utah citizens (Ackerman 2014). Representative Roberts sponsored Utah House Bill 161, *Prohibition on Electronic Data Collection Assistance* that restricts Utah from assisting the Federal Government surveillance activities through material support (Roberts 2014). The bill was defeated on 13 March 2014 (Utah State Legislature 2014).

The California State Assembly proposed *Senate Bill-828 Assistance to Federal Agencies* that prohibits the State of California from providing any assistance to a federal agency that collects or stores any information that is illegal or unconstitutional

(California State Senate Rules Committee 2014). If passed, the bill will ban the State of California from providing any form of assistance to the National Security Agency's data center in Utah, to include electrical power, water, and university partnerships (Value Walk Staff 2014). The bill passed in the California Assembly on 21 August 2014 and passed the California State Senate on 28 August 2014. The State Senate submitted the bill to the California Governor on 4 September 2014 (California Legislature 2014). Proponents expect the bill to further debate on the Foreign Intelligence Surveillance Court processes and the information that the National Security Agency collects on United States citizens and non-citizens that reside in the United States (Value Walk Staff 2014).

The House of Representatives passed *House Resolution 3361-USA Freedom Act* on 22 May 2014 with a vote of 303 to 121 (U.S. House of Representatives 2014). The bill has widespread support with 152 co-sponsors from both conservative and liberal politicians supporting the measure. If passed, the law will revise the existing processes that the intelligence community must follow when gathering information on American citizens (U.S. House of Representatives 2014). The Senate has two additional bills awaiting consideration regarding the same subject (U.S. House of Representatives 2014).

On 17 January 2014, President Obama delivered a speech regarding a review of signals intelligence (White House Press Secretary 2014). The President changed the existing policy on collecting telephone metadata by moving collection efforts from three steps away from a target to only two. This change will assist in protecting privacy rights by reducing the amount of metadata collected on distant parties. The President also directed review, reform, and potential redesign of the intelligence collection efforts to improve the protection of privacy and civil liberties while still gathering the required information to protect the United States from terrorist activities (White House Press Secretary 2014).

Support for the Intelligence Collection Efforts

Inside Cybersecurity published the article "Obama's top military adviser urges new federal cybersecurity rules," on 18 September 2014. In the article, General Martin Dempsey, the Chairman of the Joint Chiefs of Staff, feels that the United States needs to do more to protect cyberspace, but needs to balance between privacy, transparency, and security. According to General Dempsey, "there's a huge debate about whether the central government should impose standards on cyber and if they do, won't it in some way undermine the very nature of the—the wonder of the Internet, which is openness" (Castelli 2014). The current administration's policy is to encourage participation in voluntary cyber security standards. However, no one agency is in charge of protecting everything cyberspace and the collaboration between those agencies is voluntary and not standardized (Castelli 2014).

On 1 August 2013, the United States House of Representatives Permanent Select Committee on Intelligence released a statement regarding oversight of the *Foreign Intelligence Surveillance Act*. In part, that statement stated that the committee understood the concerns of the American people and the privacy rights that they value. The committee is looking for ways to improve transparency and protect privacy while still enabling intelligence programs to be effective. "Both of our Committees are conducting lengthy discussions with the Executive Branch and privacy advocates in developing initial ideas, and we look forward to discussing these proposals with the President today" (U.S. House of Representatives Permanent Select Committee on Intelligence 2013).

Literature Review Summary

The literature reviewed as part of this study shows a set of strategies, policies, and laws that are often confused with no clear agency in charge. Congress wrote laws to prosecute crimes committed within the United States borders, and defined military actions outside those same borders. Cyberspace confuses both as it cuts across internal and external borders. Events in cyberspace cannot be definitively determined to be the act of a transnational criminal organization, a terrorist organization, or a nation state sponsoring an act of war. The speed of cyberspace requires a quick response to defend the nation. However, without a clear agency in charge of transnational cyberspace attacks, counterproductive actions, confusion, or inaction are the likely responses.

CHAPTER 3

RESEARCH METHODOLOGY

Some people like to contend that there is a "sovereignty problem" on the Internet, that because no one own cyberspace in its entirety, no one has any responsibility for its integrity or security.`
— Richard A. Clarke and Robert K. Knake, *Cyber War*

The design of this study is a qualitative analysis of case studies looking at various aspects of the cyberspace security problem. The research examines national level strategy and policy as related to these case studies with the intent of determining what is possible in the current legal, political, and citizen-acceptable realms. The analysis and conclusion are based on:

1. An analysis of the national level strategies for security and defense of

   cyberspace in the United States to include:

   a. United States national level strategy and policies that address the

      protection of cyberspace

   b. Department level strategy and policies that address the protection of

      cyberspace

   c. The roles and responsibilities of the Departments of Homeland Security

      and Defense in the protection of cyberspace at it relates to homeland

      security

   d. The roles and responsibilities of the Departments of Homeland Security

      and Defense in the protection of cyberspace at it relates to homeland

      defense

e. Consistency of the homeland security and homeland defense strategies

   and policies as they interface, overlap, and/or create a gap in protection

   of cyberspace

2. A comparison of the cyberspace response forces of the Departments of

   Homeland Security and Defense to include:

   a. Examination of the policy and procedures that connect the processes

      together allowing for an integrated response to a transnational

      cyberspace attack

   b. Examination of the capabilities of the Departments of Homeland

      Security and Defense in responding to a transnational cyberspace attack

   c. Examination of other United States government agencies that may have

      a role protecting the United States from transnational cyberspace attack

3. Identification of the legal limitations on the use of cyberspace forces to respond

   to transnational cyberspace attacks including:

   a. Examination of the Department of Homeland Security's legal

      responsibilities and legal limitations regarding transnational cyberspace

      attacks

   b. Examination of the Department of Defense's legal responsibilities and

      legal limitations regarding transnational cyberspace attacks

4. Third party analysis examines the acceptability and suitability of the current

   United States Government roles, responsibilities, and responses including:

   a. The public's acceptance or rejection of the Federal Government's role

      in the defense and security of cyberspace

b. The roles and responsibilities of the private sector in the defense and

security of cyberspace

c. Demonstrated success, failure, strength, and weakness of approaches to

cyberspace breaches within the United States and the public reaction to

those breaches

A table compares the similarities and differences between three separate incidents. Several articles and Federal Government strategies report information that led to the metrics, their answers, and the relevance of that information. Table 3 shows the framework for this comparison.

Metric	Definition of answer	Relevance
	Table 3. Case Study Methodology	
Payment cards exposed / people with personal information exposed [a]	How many payment cards were exfiltrated? [a] How many people had personally identifiable information exposed? [a]	Less is better [a]
Date of breach [a]	When did the attackers first gain entry into the victim network? [a]	Known date attack started [a]
Date breach contained [a]	When was the exfiltration of information stopped? [a]	Date company stopped the breach, regardless of the use of the affected system(s) [a]
Time information exposed [a]	How long was the vulnerability present that allowed the information to be exfiltrated? [a]	less time is better [a]
Corporation stance [a]	Did the corporation that controlled the victim network maintain an active or passive network security posture? [a]	Active is better [a]
Information encryption [a]	Did the corporations protect information by using encryption? [a]	Yes is better [a]
Countries involved in data exfiltration and/or exploitation [b]	Which countries were involved in the exfiltration or exploitation of data? [b]	Less countries is better [b]
Attack vector [a]	How did the hackers gain access into the victim network? [a]	More protection is better [a]
Department of Homeland Security response [c]	What sections of Department of Homeland Security responded? [c]	Several sections may be involved [c]
Department of Justice response [d]	What sections of Department of Justice responded? [d]	Several sections may be involved [d]
Department of Defense / National security Administration response [e]	What sections of Department of Defense responded? [e]	Several sections may be involved [e]
Other federal agency/department response [f]	What other federal entities responded? [f]	Several sections may be involved [f]
Estimated loss [g]	What is the estimated damage in the victim corporation, account holders, banks and other stakeholders in United States dollars? [g]	Less cost is better [g]

Source: Information adopted from [a] U. S. Senate Committee on Commerce, Science, and Transportation, "A 'Kill Chain' Analysis of the 2013 Target Data Breach," 26 March 2014, 1-3, accessed 10 September 2014, http://www.commerce.senate.gov/public/ ?a=Files.Serve&File_id=24d3c229-4f2f-405d-b8db-a3a67f183883; [b] U. S. Senate Committee on Commerce, Science, and Transportation, "A 'Kill Chain' Analysis of the 2013 Target Data Breach," 26 March 2014, 11-12, accessed 10 September 2014, http://www.commerce.senate.gov/public/?a=Files.Serve&File_id=24d3c229-4f2f-405d-

b8db-a3a67f183883; [c] U.S. Department of Homeland Security, "National Cyber Incident Response Plan" Interim Version, September 2010, 4-5, accessed 21 September 2014, http://www.federalnewsradio.com/pdfs/NCIRP_Interim_Version_September_2010.pdf; [d] The Attorney General, *Department of Justice Strategic Plan*, 2013, 13-14, accessed 4 September 2014, http://www.justice.gov/jmd/strategic2014-2018/doj-fy-2014-2018-strategic-plan.pdf; [e] U. S. Department of Defense, *Strategy for Operating in Cyberspace*, July 2011, 8-10, accessed 20 September 2014, http://www.defense.gov/news/d20110714cyber.pdf; [f] U.S. President, *The National Strategy to Secure Cyberspace*, February, 55-60, accessed 24 March 2014, http://georgewbush-whitehouse.archives.gov/pcipb/; [g] Brian Krebs "The Target Breach, By the Numbers," *Krebs on Security*, 6 May 2014, accessed 24 September 2014, http://krebsonsecurity.com/2014/05/the-target-breach-by-the-numbers/.

A single case study might be viewed as an anomaly rather than a wide spread problem. However, comparisons of several case studies help reveal similarities and weaknesses in the current security stance of protection of payment card information (Baxter and Jack 2008, 550). To mitigate the view that a single case study may not properly represent a wider problem, three case studies are used. Multiple case studies allow the examination of storing, processing, and securing payment card information from different perspectives (Creswell 2007, 129). This study examines three different incidents from the perspective of three different industries: payments processing, multimedia, and retail sales. The cases chosen represent the diversity of corporations and the international aspect of the payment card systems.

Each of the cases examined demonstrates the diversity of the problem securing payment card information (Creswell 2007, 129). The case of Target's network breach in 2013 highlights the vulnerabilities of the point-of-sale terminals and the security vulnerabilities of using outside contractors. Sony's network breach in 2011 demonstrates the transnational nature of information storage as well as the vulnerabilities associated with complex infrastructures. The Heartland Payment Systems incident of 2008 shows how a company whose sole purpose is the storage, transfer, and use of information can have security practices with significant vulnerabilities. In each of these cases, the company's state, or purport, to follow the industry accepted security practices. However, those standards did not ensure the protection of the payment card information.

Table 3 captures the cyberspace security climate at Target, Sony, and Heartland Payment Systems at the time of the breach. This comparison shows the time of the breach, the size, and scope of the breach, and the involvement of both the public sector and the Federal Government when the breach took place. A comparison of the reaction to the breach is crucial to determine if the current policies and procedures are adequate, or if adjustments are required.

The number of payment cards and personal information exposed, how long the vulnerability existed on the victim network, and the estimated loss of the event are useful in comparing the scope of incidents. Higher numbers in these categories indicate more severe problems with lower numbers more desirable.

Company security at the time of the breach is important to understand what could have been done prior to and during the cyber-attack. The dates when the breach began and when the breach was contained are useful in understanding the nature of the problem. Information exposed for a longer time indicates that the victim company was not aware of the problem, unable to stop the incident, and/or unconcerned with customer information. The corporation stance is a related metric that describes the company's culture of network security at the time of the incident. Proactive security that was looking for problems is preferred to an approach that waits for an attack to take place.

59

Encryption of information is a protective measure that denies the information to the hackers even if they successfully extract the data out of the victim network. If victim corporations do not encrypt their information, hackers are able to use that information immediately without additional processing. Encrypted information is not valuable to hackers, but unencrypted information is very valuable.

The number of countries involved is a measure of the difficulty of law enforcement efforts. Investigations become much more complex when additional nations are involved. Each nation has its own laws regarding the sharing of information and the willingness to cooperate with the United States. A lower number of countries allows for easier investigations as there is less international coordination and cooperation required.

The attack vector is a display of the method that hackers used to gain access to the victim network. Commonalities may indicate where national efforts can focus to achieve the most gain for the effort expended. Vectors that attack publically accessible systems indicate weaknesses in external Internet security while vectors into internal networks indicate inside actor threats. Internal networks are easier to protect and offer better security making them more desirable.

The Secret Service and Federal Bureau of Investigation should be involved in each of these case studies. However, this study does not make that assumption. Other federal department may be involved with the investigation as well. The four categories of federal agency involvement capture the whole-of-government approach for each of the case studies.

Department of Defense and National Security Agency cyberspace capabilities are classified as seen by the declassified and redacted Foreign Surveillance Intelligence

Court documents (Office of the Assistant Attorney General, 2004). Before declassification, these documents were Top Secret. The Office of the Director of National Intelligence continues to redact the tactics, techniques, and procedures used to protect systems and infrastructure when these documents are released (Savage 2014). Intelligence activities governed by United States Code Title 50 protect this information and are not available to the public. Due to the restrictions of cyberspace operations information, this study will focus on those aspects of policy and procedures that are unclassified in nature and available through open sources.

The final portion of this study analyses the gaps of policy, strategy, and law. Chapter 5 lists recommendations to mitigate those gaps to improve protection of cyberspace and the economy. The recommendations compare where the policy would best serve the common good of the defense and security of cyberspace. The multinational problem of cyberspace places challenges on any law enforcement or military action as each has separate roles and responsibilities regarding security and defense of the United States. However, the United States can make changes that comply with our nations laws to both protect the nation and maintain privacy rights of our citizens.

CHAPTER 4

ANALYSIS

The reality is that a major cyber-attack from another nation is likely to originate in the U.S., so we will not be able to see it coming and block it with the systems we have now or those that are planned.

— Richard A. Clarke and Robert K. Knake, *Cyber War*

Introduction

This study examines three cases of cyber-attacks. These case studies demonstrate the challenges of operating within the Internet. The numerous vulnerabilities present challenges to companies who process, store, or transmit payment card information. Yet, this is necessary to accept credit and debit cards in lieu of cash. In each of these cases, industry certification of some form was a requirement to accept the payment cards. Each of these cases also involved international aspects to commit the crimes. Finally, the response from the Federal Government was reactive in each of the cases. The author chose these case studies to demonstrate the challenges and opportunities of securing payment card information, as well as the methods the United States employs to ensure the economy will continue to function.

Target Corporation Breach, 2013

On 18 December 2013, Brian Krebs, a computer security reporter for Krebs on Security, reported the breach of Target's systems and the exposure of credit and debit card information of millions of its customers (Krebs 2013b). Target confirmed the report a day later stating that criminals compromised 40-million payment cards. As the details of the events unfolded, the extent of the damage grew with up to an additional 70-million customers' personal information stolen in addition to the payment card information (Target Brands Inc. 2014b).

Target is a security conscious company that has implemented systems to protect its computer networks and the information they hold. The retail giant installed a FireEye computer security system that completed a month long testing phase in May 2013. The system was designed to detect attacks inside the retail network by simulating a parallel virtual computer environment that would fool hackers into thinking they were breaching the real network. The FireEye system would observe hackers attacking the imaginary network and stop the attack before they reached any critical information. The system would automatically respond to protect the network by removing malware automatically. However, Target network security disabled that option (Riley et al. 2014).

Attacks began about two months prior to the retail store infection far away from any Target store. Fazio Mechanical is a heating, ventilation, and air conditioning company in Sharpsburg, Pennsylvania, that had contracts with Target. As an authorized vendor, Fazio had access to Target's network in the form of Microsoft Active Directory credentials to allow access to several software systems, including an external billing system called *Ariba*, that Target used to issue payments. In addition to the external connection, the *Ariba* system also had an internal connection to Target's network to allow Target system administrators to maintain the system. Through these connections, the Active Directory credentials granted to Fazio allowed access to systems on Target's internal network.

Fazio was the first victim in a series of cyberspace attacks that led to Target. The heating company used a free version of *Malwarebytes Antivirus* to protect itself from infection. However, the free version of this software does not possess automatic scanning features (Malwarebytes Corporation 2014), leaving the company vulnerable to many software infections. Without the automation, malware can slip by without detection. Frazio likely received malware called *Citadel* through a malicious electronic mail. This software steals passwords and is capable of obtaining the Microsoft Active Directory credentials issued by Target. Fazio was probably not the intended target, but was a critical link in the security chain when the *Citadel* malware obtained the network credentials. Once the Active Directory credentials were exposed, it gave the attackers a tool to use against the retail giant. Internet searches revealed Fazio's contract with Target (Krebs 2014c). An announcement posted on Fazio's website states that the company complies with industry security practices and was merely a victim in this unfortunate incident (Riley et al. 2014).

Attackers distributed the majority of the malware to Target's point of sale systems between 15 and 28 November 2013. Installed *Symantec Antivirus* software detected unusual behavior on the network beginning on 28 November 2013, but these alerts did not result in any response by Target's network security staff (U.S. Senate Committee on Commerce, Science, and Transportation 2013, 3).

Attackers installed additional software on 30 November 2013 to a Target server, to aid them in moving information from the point of sale systems. The assailants designed the software to bypass network security and firewalls, and move information out of Target's network. The criminals updated this software twice on 2 December 2013. Target's FireEye system sent an "urgent alert" each time the server software was installed (U.S. Senate Committee on Commerce, Science, and Transportation 2013, 3). However,

64

Target's security team did not respond to these indications either (U.S. Senate Committee on Commerce, Science, and Transportation 2013, 3). By responding to the security alerts, the security team could have disabled the malware and prevented attackers from removing information. Security firm Seculert analyzed the malware and much of the logs related to the Target breach, and determined that data exfiltration did not begin until 2 December 2014 (Raff 2014).

The malware exploited a weakness in Target's internal networks, which allowed it to install itself on Target's cash registers, or point-of-sale systems, through the stores located in the United States. Once installed, the malware read the memory of the affected point-of-sale system, found the unencrypted payment card information, and forwarded the information to a server within Target's infrastructure (U.S. Senate Committee on Commerce, Science, and Transportation 2013, 2). According to computer security journalist, Brian Krebs, the malware, which ran on a version of Microsoft Windows, appears to be a modified version of the *BlackPOS* malware. The software is available for sale on the Internet for as low as $1,800. The modified *BlackPOS* software allowed the malware to hide from over forty different commercially available antivirus tools (Krebs 2014a).

The malicious software gathered credit card numbers and encrypted Personal Identification Numbers (PIN) from debit cards, and sent the information from the infected point-of-sale systems to an infected Target server once an hour. After the malware sent the information, it deleted the information from the point-of-sale systems (Harris et al. 2014). Six days later, the Target server sent the information to an infected web server and then off to Russia (Harris et al. 2014). Sources do not agree on the exact flow of information from Target's network to external actors. Krebs reports that servers located in Miami, Florida and in Brazil held the information before sending it onto Russia (Krebs 2014b). However, Michael Riley's more recent article reports three servers located in Ashburn, Virginia, Provo Utah, and Los Angeles, California (Riley et al. 2014). Riley and others report that Odessa, Ukraine received the information before forwarding it onto Moscow, Russia (Riley et al. 2014).

In addition to the payment cards, personal information was also exfiltrated from Target's network. However, it is unclear how this attack took place (U.S. Senate Committee on Commerce, Science, and Transportation 2013). Target reported the exposure of personal information on as many as 70-million customers. The information at risk included personal information such as electronic mail addresses and phone numbers (Target Brands Inc. 2014b).

Target Chief Financial Officer and Executive Vice President, John Mulligan, testified before the Senate Committee on the Judiciary on 4 February 2014 that Target first found out about the credit card breach on 12 December 2013 when the Department of Justice contacted them requesting a meeting (U.S. Senate Committee on Commerce, Science, and Transportation 2013, 1). Target held the meeting the following day with the Department of Justice, and the Secret Service in attendance (Harris et al. 2014). Mister Mulligan also testified that Target was certified by the Payment Card Industry Data Security Standards in September 2013, as required by credit card companies, and had "in place multiple layers of protection, including firewalls, malware detection software, intrusion detection and prevention capabilities and data loss prevention tools" (United States Senate Committee on Commerce, Science, and Transportation 2013, 7).

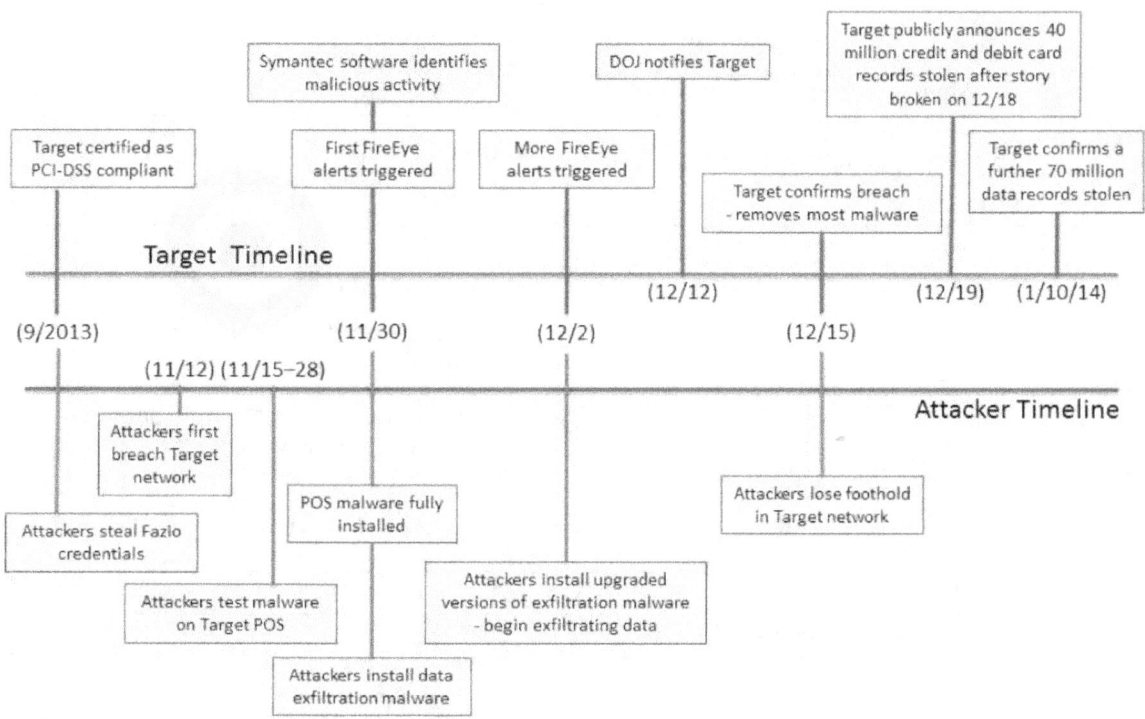

Figure 1.   A Timeline of the Target Data Breach

Source: United States Senate Committee on Commerce, "A "Kill Chain" Analysis of the 2013 Target Data Breach," 2013, 12, accessed 10 September 2014, http://www.commerce.senate.gov/public/?a=Files.Serve&File_id=24d3c229-4f2f-405d-b8db-a3a67f183883.

Table 4.

Metric	Measurement
Payment cards exposed / people with personal information exposed	40 million [a]/ up to 70 million [a]
Date of breach	15 November 2013 [b]
Date breach contained	15 December 2013 [a]
Time data exposed	30 days
Corporation stance	Security systems installed, but not monitored [c], security practices compliant with industry standards [b]
Information encryption status	Unencrypted payment cards, personal information, and unencrypted debit card PINs [a]
Countries involved in data exfiltration and/or exploitation	United States, [a] Ukraine, [c] Russia, [d] Brazil [e]
Attack vector	Point of sale system [d] through vendor payment system [f]
Department of Homeland Security response	Secret Service investigation [a]
Department of Justice response	Department of Justice investigation [a]
Department of Defense response	None reported
Other federal response	None reported
Estimated loss	$404.3M [g]

Table 4. Target Breach 2013

Source: Data adopted from [a] Target Brands Incorporated, "data breach FAQ," accessed 24 September 2014, https://corporate.target.com/about/shopping-experience/payment-card-issue-FAQ.aspx#q6270; [b] United States Senate Committee on Commerce, Science, and Transportation, "A 'Kill Chain' Analysis of the 2013 Target Data Breach," 26 March 2014, accessed 10 September 2014, http://www.commerce.senate.gov/public/?a=Files.Serve&File_id=24d3c229-4f2f-405d-b8db-a3a67f183883; [c] Michael Riley et al., "Missed Alarms and 40 Million Stolen Credit Card Numbers: How Target Blew It," *Bloomberg Businessweek*, 13 March 2014, accessed 14 March 2014, http://www.businessweek.com/articles/2014-03-13/target-missed-alarms-in-epic-hack-of-credit-card-data; [d] Nart Villeneuve, "Where have all the credit cards gone? The cyber-crime underground and its ties to Eastern Europe," *FireEye Blog*, 3 February 2014, accessed 24 September 2014, http://www.fireeye.com/blog/corporate/2014/02/where-have-all-the-credit-cards-gone-the-cyber-crime-underground-and-its-ties-to-eastern-europe.html; [e] Brian Krebs, "Target Hackers Broke in Via HVAC Company," *Krebs on Security*, 5 February 2014, accessed 24 September 2014, http://krebsonsecurity.com/2014/02/target-hackers-broke-in-via-hvac-company/; [f] Brian Krebs, "Email Attack on Vendor Set Up Breach at Target," *Krebs on Security*, 12 February 2014, accessed 24 September 2014, http://krebsonsecurity.com/2014/02/email-attack-on-vendor-set-up-breach-at-target/; [g] Data compiled from Rachel Abrams, "Target Puts Data Breach Costs at $148 Million, and Forecasts Profit Drop," *The New York Times*, 5 August 2014, accessed 24 September 2014, http://www.nytimes.com/2014/08/06/business/target-puts-data-breach-costs-at-148-million.html; Associated Press, "Target Data Breach Cost for Banks Tops $200M," *NBC News*, 18 February 2014, accessed 24 September 2014, http://www.nbcnews.com/business/business-news/target-data-breach-cost-banks-tops-200m-n33156; Brian Krebs "The Target Breach, By the Numbers," *Krebs on Security*, 6 May 2014, accessed 24 September 2014, http://krebsonsecurity.com/2014/05/the-target-breach-by-the-numbers/

Verizon and Mandiant, computer experts called in to remediate Target's networks, studied the computer and firewall logs, and other computer forensics to determine how to stop and mitigate the damage. Security experts cleaned Target's networks by removing the malware from all the systems, changing the passwords, and examining the network security in detail (Harris et al. 2014).

The Secret Service confirmed that it has an ongoing investigation into the Target breach (Stock 2013). However, little additional information is available. The Secret Service has visited Target (U.S. Senate Committee on Commerce, Science, and Transportation 2013, 1), and Fazio Mechanical in the course of its investigation (Krebs 2014b). Evidence also points to the Secret Service monitoring the sale of stolen credit card information in Odessa, Ukraine (Riley et al. 2014), which may be how The Justice Department and the Secret Service knew of the attack before Target did.

Similarly, few details are available on the Department of Justice or the Federal Bureau of Investigation involvement in the 2013 Target breach. However, the Department of Justice has been involved internationally with other similar incidents. In the mid-2000s, the Department of Justice requested European assistance to shut down a company called Carderplanet for selling stolen credit card information (Riley et al. 2014).

Target's cost of the breach resulted in $148 million in actual expenses, so far. Insurance coverage is expected cover as much as $38 million of that cost (Abrams 2014). What is not easily measurable is the amount of revenue Target will lose due to reduced sales resulting from customers' lack of trust in Target's security. The total damage to the Target, financial institutions, and customers is much higher. The Consumer Bankers Associate estimates the cost of reissuing cards for its members at $172 million. The Credit Union National Association's estimate is $30.6 million (Associated Press 2014a). Krebs estimates one to three million cards will sell on the black market for an estimated price of $53.7 million (Krebs 2014d).

The author believes that the $53.7 million estimate may be a low estimate of fraudulent charges against the cards. Criminals will purchase the cards with the intention of making fraudulent purchases and will expect to get more than they paid for the cards. A combination of cardholders and card issuing institutions will likely pay these costs. In either case, this will increase the total cost of the breach. Adding up these estimates and actual figures, the total expected cost of the 2013 Target breach is over $404.3 million.

Related to the breach, and in an effort to protect payment card and transaction information, Target has accelerated its plans by six months to upgrade its point-of-sale systems to accept newer and more secure payment cards, often referred to as chip-and-pin. These payment cards contain an embedded computer chip that encrypts the transaction information from the card itself. Target will continue to accept the more traditional magnetic strip cards. However, the new point-of-sale terminals will allow customers the option of using more secure technology as well (Target Brands Inc. 2014a).

Sony Breach, 2011

In April 2011, Sony's PlayStation, Qriocity, and Sony Online Entertainment networks were the victim of cyber-attacks (Sony Online Entertainment 2011). The attacks compromised the personal and financial payment information on 101-million accounts (Haselton 2011) and cost the multimedia company over $171 million (Dignan 2011).

Prior events may have contributed to the Sony network breaches. On 11 January 2011 (Reisinger 2011a), Sony filed a restraining order against a computer programmer, George Hotz, for designing and distributing software that defeated encryption standards, and allowed PlayStation owners to hack into their gaming consoles to use unapproved, or possibly pirated, software (S 2011). Judge Susan Illston of the United States District Court for the Northern District of California granted the restraining order on 26 January 2011 due, in part, to a violation of the *Digital Millennium Copyright Act* (U.S. District Court for the Northern District of California 2011).

The hacking activist, or hacktivist, organization Anonymous noticed the legal action against Hotz and began denial-of-service attacks on Sony's enterprise (Sherr and Wingfield 2011). Sony reported the first incident on 4 April 2011 (Kill 2011). Sony did not acknowledge the problems as attacks and instead responded with the statement, "[PlayStation networks] are currently undergoing sporadic maintenance. Access to the [PlayStation networks] may be interrupted throughout the day. We apologize for any inconvenience" (Daily Mail Reporter 2011). The Author believes this to be a typical industry-response to hacking, as companies do not want to alarm users or lose customer confidence by demonstrating a lack of security or resilience in their networks.

71

Anonymous claimed partial responsibility for some of these Sony attacks. Xavier Monsegur, an Anonymous connected hacker, and one of the notable leaders of the connected hacktivist group LulzSec, admitted to the Federal Bureau of Investigation his involvement with breaking into Sony as well as the Public Broadcasting system, and Bethesda Softworks (Westervelt 2014). These attacks happened at about the same time as the breach into Sony's networks. However, Anonymous and Lulzsec attacks historically degrade networks rather than remove information. In the process of trying to limit Sony's networks, the hacktivist attacks may have provided some unintentional cover for the attackers to hide their activities.

Sony engineers discovered the breach to the PlayStation network while troubleshooting an unusual problem with servers continually shutting down and restarting (Sherr and Wingfield 2011). The technicians discovered four servers in an AT&T data center in San Diego, California (Miller 2011) repeatedly dropping off line on 19 April 2011. Technicians disabled the four servers, out of a total of one-hundred-and-thirty to contain the problem (Sherr and Wingfield 2011). The following day, the team found indications that an intruder had been inside of the network. Technicians shut down all PlayStation servers to prevent any additional hacker activity. On 20 April 2011, Sony contacted the first of three security companies to assist with clean-up efforts. The following day, Sony hired the second security company to assist. On 22 April 2011, Sony finally posted on its PlayStation Blog that an intrusion had taken place (Schaaff 2011). On the same day, Sony contacted the Federal Bureau of Investigation to aid in the analysis. By 23 April 2011, details surfaced that the hackers had obtained access to restricted areas of the PlayStation network and attempted to hide their activity (Sherr and

Wingfield 2011). The investigation continued on 24 April 2011 with a third security firm brought into the investigation to determine the scope of the problem (Schaaff 2011).

Two days later, Patrick Seybold, Sony's Senior Director of Corporate Communications and Social Media, posted on a PlayStation blog explaining the breach, between 17 and 19 April 2011, of both the PlayStation gaming network and the Qriocity music and video service. In that post, Sony disclosed that hackers compromised customer accounts. Attackers had accessed personal information that customers had posted on the sites including account login name and password, network handle, customer name, address, phone number, electronic mail address, physical mailing address, and birthdate. Access to additional information was unclear such as purchase history, billing address, security questions, and answers, and credit card number and expiration date. The credit card security codes were not exposed (Sony Computer Entertainment and Sony Network Entertainment 2011). The attacks exposed information from 77-million customers in 59 countries: 36-million from the United States, 32-million from Europe, and 9-million from Asia (Robertson and Nakashima 2011).

On 1 May 2011, Sony revealed the breach of Sony Online Entertainment as well. Sony shut down this service the following day (Schaaff 2011). In this connected attack, hackers gained access to 24.6-million user accounts including the credit card numbers from 12,700 users from the United States, and 10,700 direct debit records of some users in Austria, Germany, The Netherlands, and Spain (Sony Online Entertainment 2011). The newly discovered breach brought the total victim count to 101-million accounts compromised and an estimated 12.3-million credit card numbers revealed (Haselton

2011). The attack, and the protective actions taken by Sony to contain the breach, resulted in the PlayStation gaming network shut down for 40 days (BBC News 2011b).

Unknown actors were responsible for hacking Sony's networks. However, Kevin Poulsen has excluded some organizations as suspects. Anonymous, as an organization, has not shown interest in removing information, instead denying access to corporate systems (Poulsen 2011). Supporting this line of thought, Anonymous released a statement on 4 May 2014 claiming no responsibility in the data removal attacks (Sherr and Wingfield 2011). Chinese hackers have shown interest in taking information, but have focused on corporate and military espionage rather than personal or financial information, excluding them as suspects as well. Poulsen feels the most likely organizations to be at the root of the PlayStation hack are involved in financial crime. Many of these criminals reside in Russia and Ukraine (Poulsen 2011).

On 28 April 2011, United States Senator Richard Blumenthal from Connecticut sent a letter to Attorney General, Eric Holder requesting an investigation of Sony, and the breach of their networks. The letter specifically addressed the time Sony took to notify affected users (Blumenthal 2011). No reports are available from the Department of Justice explaining their investigation of Sony. However, Federal Bureau of Investigation agent Darrell Foxworth confirmed that the Bureau was reviewing information to determine any criminal activity (Webster 2011).

At a Tokyo news conference delivered by Sony executives on 1 May 2011 (Caplin 2011), Mister Shinji Hasejima, Senior Vice President and Chief Information Officer of Sony, explained that the hackers hid their activities by mimicking normal transactions that firewalls could not distinguish from normal Internet traffic (Hirai,

Hasejima and Kambe 2011). Sony released the following diagram, shown as figure 2 below, during the news conference. The diagram depicts, generically, how hackers were able to get at the personal information through the network infrastructure. Sony has not revealed what vulnerabilities were present on the network, firewalls, web server, application server, or the database server (Veracode 2011).

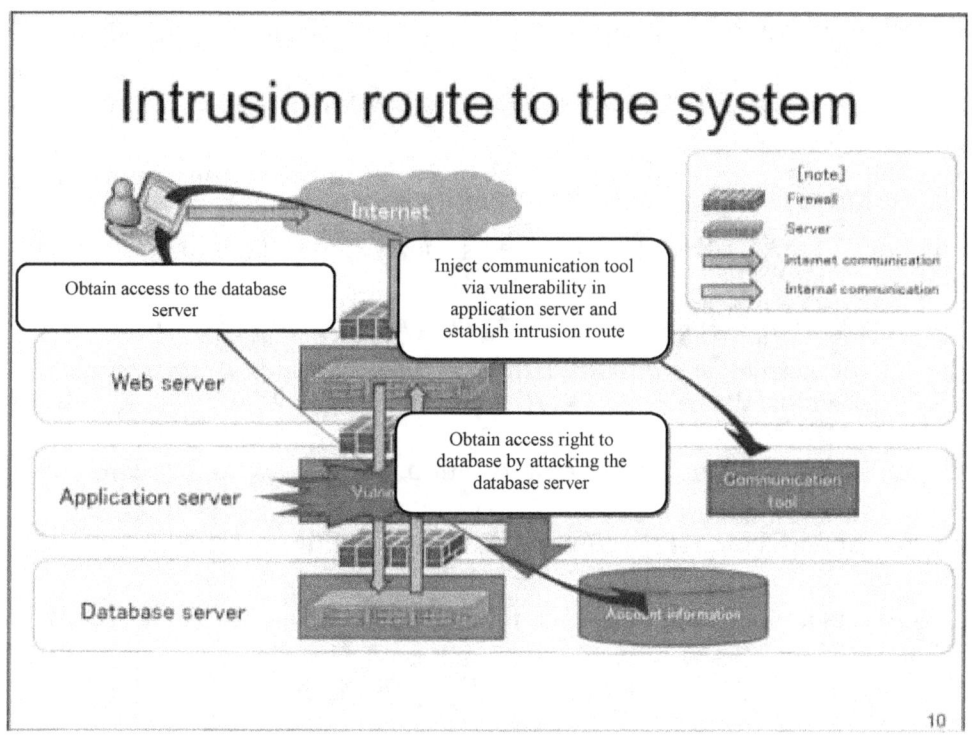

Figure 2.   Intrusion Route to PlayStation Network

Source: Semiconportal, "Sony asks FBI to investigate unauthorized network intrusion," 2 May 2011, accessed 28 September 2014, https://www.semiconportal.com/en/ archive/news/main-news/110502-sony-network-intrusion.html.

Speculation on how hackers were able to get into the PlayStation network has surrounded Sony's release of the *Rebug* software earlier in the year. The software, released on 3 March 2011, allows developers to explore the software and hardware capabilities of the PlayStation 3 gaming system. This software allows for additional capabilities that normal users do not have (Kerner 2011). Veracode, in their article, "Possible PlayStation Network Attack Vectors," explains that *Rebug* allowed hackers to connect a PlayStation 3 to an unexpected part of the PlayStation network, allowing users to gain unlimited credit to an account without the system validating with a credit card. This one example of the unintended capabilities of the *Rebug* software shows that Sony was not aware of the vulnerabilities this software introduced into their network. There were forty-five instances of the PlayStation network at the time of the Sony breach. Veracode posits that several of these networks were for internal Sony users only. It is possible that one of these networks contained security flaws that allowed users to get past one or more firewalls within the PlayStation network (Veracode 2011). However it happened, hackers gained access to the network and were able to install a communication tool on the applications sever. This communication tool allowed information to flow out of the firewalls and to the Internet without suspicion (Semiconportal 2011). Database and application servers are normally designed to communicate together to share information. The author believes it is likely that access to the application server provided direct, or nearly direct, access to the sensitive information the thieves were attempting to obtain.

On 16 May 2011, Bloomberg ran an article regarding Amazon's involvement in the Sony breach. In the article "Sony Network Breach Shows Amazon Cloud's Appeal for Hackers," Amazon's Elastic Computer Cloud (EC2) service played a role in hacking the PlayStation Network. Hackers used a fictitious name to set up an Amazon account granting access to the servers. Sony, Amazon, and the Federal Bureau of Investigation would not comment on how the servers aided hackers in the PlayStation breach. The

Elastic Computer Cloud service allows businesses to expand their data center with minimal investment. However, nefarious actors can use it as well (Galante, Kharif, and Alpeyev 2011).

The large-scale breach begs questions regarding the security posture of Sony and the management of both its information technology, and the information itself. Visa and MasterCard post lists of companies that are compliant with the Payment Card Industry Data Security Standards. These standards outline minimum-security considerations to store, transmit, and retain payment and customer information. Neither Visa nor MasterCard listed Sony among the list of security compliant companies in their September and November 2011 reports (Klemic 2012, 10). Also notably missing is Sony mentioning compliance in numerous press releases and legal proceedings. Evidence points to poor security practices by Sony as demonstrated by the retention of an old and outdated payment card database (Chung 2013). To be compliant with Payment Card Industry Data Security Standards, Sony should have destroyed this database when no longer needed. However, Sony did not follow that industry standard (Klemic 2012, 8-11).

The breach of Sony's PlayStation, Qriocity, and Sony Online Entertainment networks resulted in substantial costs to the multi-media company. In the United Kingdom, the Information Commissioner's Office found that Sony failed to protect user information within Sony's networks (Westervelt 2014) and fined Sony £250,000, or about $396,100, for failing to provide proper network security practices to protect private and financial information (BBC News 2013).

Similarly, the Southern District of the United States District Court declared a preliminary ruling against Sony on 10 July 2014 on a class action lawsuit filed by several plaintiffs (Grande 2014). The ruling will cost Sony $15 million in payments and services to affected class members (Lien 2014). In addition to the $15 million settlement, the lawsuit also requires Sony to pay for $2.75 million in attorney's fees and up to $1.25 million to notify affected settlement members. Sony will have its final day in court on 1 May 2015 with a hearing on the case to examine if the settlement is fair and reasonable (Grande 2014).

Canadian citizen Natasha Maksimovic filed a similar case in Canada against Sony. The case requested $1 billion Canadian, or about $1.04 billion in United States dollars. (Rose 2011) Sony settled the case with damages estimated to be $1 million (Moss 2013).

Sony has spent 14 billion yen, or about $171 million, to cover costs for identify theft protection and clean up efforts to repair the network breach (Martinez 2011). However, this number will rise as customers file claims for identity theft and credit card fraud. Larry Dignan, technical reporter for ZDNet, feels that the number is only a small glimpse of what is to come with additional claims expected in the future. He anticipates a conservative estimate of Sony's damages to be around $5.6 billion (Dignan 2011). Some have felt the damages could be much higher. Jordan Robertson and Ryan Nakashima of the Associated Press reported in their article "Sony: Credit data risked in PlayStation network outage" that the average cost of credit card breaches is $318 per compromised account and estimated that damages to Sony could increase to $24 billion (Robertson and Nakashima 2011).

Since the attack, and the litigation that has resulted from the attack, Sony has updated their terms of service in an effort to mitigate damages from future intrusions.

Users must sign the new terms of service for access to the gaming network. The new terms of service, in essence, require users to give up their rights to sue as part of a class action lawsuit. Users may need to turn to arbitration to settle any disputes in the future (BBC News 2011b).

In addition to the terms of service change, Sony has also placed an emphasis on network security. As part of a pre-scheduled move, the PlayStation network moved operations from the data center in San Diego, California to a new, undisclosed, data center (Miller 2011). Sony also upgraded the PlayStation and Qriocity networks by adding automated monitoring software, data encryption, and additional firewalls (Caplin 2011).

Table 5. Sony Breach 2011	
Metric	Measurement
Payment cards exposed / people with personal information exposed	12.3 million / 101 million [a]
Date of breach	17 April 2011[b]
Date breach contained	1 May 2011 [e]
Time data exposed	14 days
Corporation stance	Reactive, [b] consumer network off-line for 40 days [c], not compliant with industry security standards
Information encryption status	Unencrypted payment cards [d] and other personal information [b]
Countries involved in data exfiltration and/or exploitation	Austria, Germany, The Netherlands, Spain [e], United States, Japan; customers in total of 59 countries [f]
Attack vector	Web server. application server, and database [g]
Department of Homeland Security response	None reported
Department of Justice response	Investigation by Federal Bureau of Investigation [h]
Department of Defense response	None reported
Other federal response	None reported
Estimated loss	$171M - $5.6B [i]

Source: Data adopted from [a] Todd Haselton, "Sony's CEO apologizes for security breach, will offer free month of PSN service," 6 May 2011, accessed 28 September 2014, http://bgr.com/2011/05/06/sonys-ceo-apologizes-for-security-breach-will-offer-free-month-of-psn-service/; [b] Sony Computer Entertainment and Sony Network Entertainment, "Update on PlayStation Network and Qriocity," *PlayStation Blog*, 26 April 2011, accessed 25 September 2014, http://blog.us.playstation.com/2011/04/26/update-on-playstation-network-and-qriocity/; [c] British Broadcasting Corporation, "Sony asks gamers to sign new terms or face PSN ban," *British Broadcasting Corporation*, 16 September 2011, accessed 28 September 2014, http://www.bbc.co.uk/news/technology-14948701; [d] Keith Stuart and Charles Arthur, "PlayStation Network hack: why it took Sony seven days to tell the world," *The Guardian,* 27 April 2011, accessed 27 September 2014, http://www.theguardian.com/technology/gamesblog/2011/apr/27/playstation-network-hack-sony; [e] Sony Online Entertainment, "Sony Online Entertainment Announces Theft of Data from Its Systems," 3 May 2011, accessed 28 September 2014, https://www.soe.com/securityupdate/pressrelease.vm; [f] Jordan Robertson and Ryan Nakashima, "Sony: Credit data risked in PlayStation network outage," *Mass Live*, 28 April 2011, accessed 25 September 2014, http://www.masslive.com/news/index.ssf/2011/04/sony_credit_data_risked_in_pla.html; [g] Semiconportal, "Sony asks FBI to investigate unauthorized network intrusion," 2 May

2011. accessed 28 September 2014, https://www.semiconportal.com/en/archive/news/ main-news/110502-sony-network-intrusion.html; [h] Andrew Webster, "FBI investigating PSN hack; Sony looking into compensating users," *Ars Technica*, 29 April 2011, accessed 28 September 2014, http://arstechnica.com/gaming/2011/04/sony-looking-into- compensating-psn-users-fbi-gets-involved/; [i] Larry Dignan, "Sony's data breach costs likely to scream higher," *ZD Net*, 24 May 2011, accessed 27 September 2014, http://www.zdnet.com/blog/btl/sonys-data-breach-costs-likely-to-scream-higher/49161.

Heartland Payment System Breach 2008

Heartland Payment Systems is a Newark, New Jersey based company that processes credit and debit card transactions on behalf of 250,000 businesses at a rate of about 100-million transactions each month (Claburn 2009). Heartland Payment Systems discovered an intrusion into their network in January 2009 (Claburn 2009), but the attack began on 26 December 2007 (Fishman 2013, 7). During that time, hackers were able to obtain information on 130-million payment cards (Krebs 2013a). Although the breach began in 2007, reports commonly refer to the incident as the 2008 Heartland breach.

Hackers exploited a vulnerability in the database language Structured Query Language, more commonly known as SQL, to gain access to Heartland's corporate network. The SQL vulnerability existed for several years prior to the attacks that compromised payment card information (Cheney 2010, 3). Attackers discovered the vulnerability on 26 December 2007 (Fishman 2013, 7) and used a method known as an SQL inject to issue unauthorized commands through a server that publically hosted web pages. These commands allowed hackers to exploit weak security on the servers and access the corporate network (Krebs 2013a).

Once inside the network, the attackers began exploring the infrastructure to determine weaknesses and discover where payment card information was stored (Prince

2009b). Hackers installed key-logger software to obtain login credentials and password, which allowed for greater access in the computer network (Claburn 2009). Attackers eventually installed sniffer software within the payment processing system to locate preferred information (Prince 2009b). The malware sought out payment card information as it moved within the network and forwarded that information outside of Heartland's network and to the hackers (Cheney 2010, 3). According to Robert Baldwin Jr., Heartland's President, and Chief Financial Officer, the software was able to obtain payment card numbers, expiration dates, and the names of the card owners (Claburn 2009).

According to the Department of Justice, servers located in California, Illinois, Latvia, The Netherlands, and Ukraine received the information (U.S. Department of Justice 2009). The indictment of Albert Gonzalez sheds some light on how the hackers operated. The United Stated indicted Albert Gonzalez, an American citizen from Miami, Florida, for his role in attacking Heartland Payment Systems' networks. Following his arrest, he explained some of the tactics used to mine the payment card information. Attackers developed software to aid in payment card removal and ensured its function by proof tested prior to deployment. Hackers ran the software through testing by attempting to detect the malware with about twenty different antivirus programs. Once the malware developers were satisfied that the software would be able to perform correctly, and hide from some standard security software, they were ready to deploy the malware in a victim network (Prince 2009b).

In addition to Mister Gonzales, the United States indicted four foreign citizens for the attack on several companies, including Heartland Payment systems. Russians Vladimir

82

Drinkman, Alexandr Kalinin, and Roman Kotov, as well as Ukrainian Mikhail Rytikov committed attacks against Heartland Payment Systems (U.S. Department of Justice 2013).

Heartland's information technology staff and external auditors conducted several inspections between December 2007 and January 2009 to certify the networks as meeting the Payments Cards Industry Digital Standards. Visa, MasterCard, Discover, American Express, and JCB all require certification to allow Heartland to process their payment cards. Qualified Security Assessors serve as outside network inspectors and routinely evaluated the security measures at Heartland. During these routine checks, Heartland was compliant with the accepted industry standards and approved to process payment-card information (Cheney 2010, 3-5). None of the compliance inspections revealed the intrusions into the networks, nor the installed malware (Cheney 2010, 7). Heartland was certified as Payment Card Industry Data Security Standard compliant in April 2008 (Claburn 2009), four months after hackers had obtained access to the network. Heartland discovered the intrusion after investigating reports of fraudulent charges from MasterCard and Visa. The reports were from businesses that Heartland was responsible for processing payments (Krebs 2009). Heartland contacted the Secret Service to aid in the investigation (Krebs 2009).

Table 6.	Heartland Payment System Breach 2008
Metric	**Measurement**
Payment cards exposed / people with personal information exposed	130 million [a] / none [b]
Date of breach	26 December 2007 [c]
Date breach contained	Discovered 12 Jan 2009 [d]
Time data exposed	Over 1 Year
Corporation stance	Reactive, after reports of possible compromise [b], certified compliant with industry security standards [e]
Information encryption status	Unencrypted payment card information [e]
Countries involved in data exfiltration and/or exploitation	United States, Latvia, The Netherlands, Ukraine [f], and Russia [g]
Attack vector	Database vulnerability on public facing web server [h]
Department of Homeland Security response	Heartland contacted Secret Service [e]
Department of Justice response	Heartland contacted Department of Justice [e]
Department of Defense response	None reported
Other federal response	Department of Treasury's Office of the Comptroller of Currency, Federal Trade Commission, and Securities and Exchange Commission [i]
Estimated loss	$200M [c]

Source: Data adopted from [a] Brian Krebs, "Hacker Ring Stole 160 Million Credit Cards," 25 July 2013, accessed 29 September 2014, http://krebsonsecurity.com/tag/heartland-payment-systems/; [b] Brian Krebs, "Payment Processor Breach May Be Largest Ever," 20 January 2009, accessed 29 September 2014, http://voices.washingtonpost.com/securityfix/2009/01/payment_processor_breach_may_b.html; [c] Paul J. Fishman, "United States of America v. Vladimir Drinkman, Aleksandr Kalinin, Roman Kotov, Mikhail Rytikov, and Dmitriy Smiliantets," 7, July 2013, accessed 29 September 2014, http://krebsonsecurity.com/wp-content/uploads/2013/07/DVKRK-Indictment.pdf; [d] Brian Prince describes the discovery of the Heartland breach during the week of 12 January 2009 and reported to the public on 20 January 2009. Brian Prince, "Heartland Payment Systems Reports Breach," 20 January 2009, accessed 29 September 2014, http://www.eweek.com/c/a/Security/Heartland-Payment-Systems-Reports-Breach/; [e] Thomas Claburn, "Heartland Payment Systems Hit By Data Security Breach," 20 January 2009, accessed 29 September 2014, http://www.darkreading.com/attacks-and-breaches/heartland-payment-systems-hit-by-data-security-breach/d/d-id/1075770?; [f] Department of Justice, "Alleged International Hacker Indicted for Massive Attack on U.S. Retail and Banking Networks," 17 August 2009, accessed 29 September 2014, http://www.justice.gov/opa/pr/alleged-international-hacker-indicted-massive-attack-us-retail-and-banking-networks; [g] Department of Justice, "Five Indicted in New Jersey for

Largest Known Data Breach Conspiracy," 25 July 2013, accessed 29 September 2014, http://www.justice.gov/opa/pr/five-indicted-new-jersey-largest-known-data-breach-conspiracy; [h] Julia S. Cheney, "Heartland Payment Systems: Lessons Learned from a Data Breach," January 2010, 3, accessed 29 September 2014, http://www.phil.frb.org/consumer-credit-and-payments/payment-cards-center/publications/discussion-papers/2010/d-2010-january-heartland-payment-systems.pdf; [i] Robert McMillan, "SEC, FTC Investigating Heartland After Data Theft," 25 February 2009, accessed 30 September 2014, http://www.pcworld.com/article/160264/heartland_investigated_by_sec_ftc.html.

The Payments Cards Industry Digital Standards required Heartland to contract out an independent forensic investigation through a certified Quality Incident Response Assessor (Cheney 2010, 7). To meet this requirement, Heartland obtained the services of two computer security firms who specialize in network breaches (Krebs 2009). It took the certified investigators six weeks to determine the cause of the network intrusion (Cheney 2010, 7).

Following the attack, Heartland stated that the company is installing increased security systems including a "next-generation program designed to flag network anomalies in real time" (Messmer 2009). However, details of what that program is, or what it does, have not been disclosed. Heartland Payment Systems lost an estimated $200 million in the attacks (Kitten 2013a).

Analysis and Comparison

Table 7 summarizes and compares the three case studies. The intent of this comparison is to evaluate the similarities and differences between the three different attacks. It also relates the scope of each of the attacks, the security stances of the affected companies, and the response from Federal Government agencies.

Metric	Target 2013	Sony 2011	Heartland 2008
Payment cards exposed / people with personal information exposed	40 million [a]/ up to 70 million [a]	12.3 million / 101 million [h]	130 million [q] / none [r]
Date of breach	15 November 2013 [b]	17 April 2011[i]	26 December 2007 [s]
Date breach contained	15 December 2013 [a]	1 May 2011 [l]	12 January 2009 [t]
Time data exposed	30 days	14 days	Over 1 Year
Corporate stance	Security systems installed, but not monitored [c], security practices compliant with industry standards [b]	Reactive [i], consumer network off-line for 40 days [j]	Reactive, after reports of compromise [r], certified compliant with industry security standards [u]
Information encryption status	Unencrypted payment cards, personal information, and unencrypted debit card PINs [a]	Unencrypted payment cards [k] and other personal information [i]	Unencrypted payment card information [u]
Countries involved in data exfiltration and/or exploitation	United States [a], Ukraine [c,] Russia [d], Brazil [e]	Austria, Germany, The Netherlands, Spain [l], United States, Japan; customers in total of 59 countries [m]	United States, Latvia, The Netherlands, Ukraine [v], and Russia [w]
Attack vector	Point of sale system [d] through vendor payment system [f]	Web server, application server, and database [n]	Database vulnerability on public facing web server [x]
Department of Homeland Security response	Secret Service investigation [a]	None reported	Heartland contacted Secret Service [u]
Department of Justice response	Department of Justice investigation [a]	Investigation by Federal Bureau of Investigation [o]	Heartland contacted Department of Justice [u]
Department of Defense response	None reported	None reported	None reported
Other federal response	None reported	None reported	Department of Treasury's Office of the Comptroller of Currency, Federal Trade Commission, and Securities and Exchange Commission [y]
Estimated loss	$404.3M [g]	$171M - $5.6B [p]	$200M [s]

Table 7. Case Study Comparison

Source: Data compiled by the author and adopted from the following sources.

Target 2013: [a] Target Brands Incorporated, "data breach FAQ," accessed 24 September 2014, https://corporate.target.com/about/shopping-experience/payment-card-issue-FAQ.aspx#q6270; [b] United States Senate Committee on Commerce, Science, and Transportation, "A 'Kill Chain' Analysis of the 2013 Target Data Breach," 26 March 2014, accessed 10 September 2014, http://www.commerce.senate.gov/public/?a=Files.Serve&File_id=24d3c229-4f2f-405d-b8db-a3a67f183883; [c] Michael Riley et al., "Missed Alarms and 40 Million Stolen Credit Card Numbers: How Target Blew It," *Bloomberg Businessweek*, 13 March 2014, accessed 14 March 2014, http://www.businessweek.com/articles/2014-03-13/target-missed-alarms-in-epic-hack-of-credit-card-data; [d] Nart Villeneuve, "Where have all the credit cards gone? The cyber-crime underground and its ties to Eastern Europe," *FireEye Blog*, 3 February 2014, accessed 24 September 2014, http://www.fireeye.com/blog/corporate/2014/02/where-have-all-the-credit-cards-gone-the-cyber-crime-underground-and-its-ties-to-eastern-europe.html; [e] Brian Krebs, "Target Hackers Broke in Via HVAC Company," *Krebs on Security,* 5 February 2014, accessed 24 September 2014, http://krebsonsecurity.com/2014/02/target-hackers-broke-in-via-hvac-company/; [f] Brian Krebs, "Email Attack on Vendor Set Up Breach at Target," *Krebs on Security*, 12 February 2014, accessed 24 September 2014, http://krebsonsecurity.com/2014/02/email-attack-on-vendor-set-up-breach-at-target/; [g] Data compiled from Rachel Abrams, "Target Puts Data Breach Costs at $148 Million, and Forecasts Profit Drop," *The New York Times*, 5 August 2014, accessed 24 September 2014, http://www.nytimes.com/2014/08/06/business/target-puts-data-breach-costs-at-148-million.html, Associated Press, "Target Data Breach Cost for Banks Tops $200M," *NBC News*, 18 February 2014, accessed 24 September 2014, http://www.nbcnews.com/business/business-news/target-data-breach-cost-banks-tops-200m-n33156; Brian Krebs, "The Target Breach, By the Numbers," *Krebs on Security*, 6 May 2014, accessed 24 September 2014, http://krebsonsecurity.com/2014/05/the-target-breach-by-the-numbers/.

Sony 2011: [h] Todd Haselton, "Sony's CEO apologizes for security breach, will offer free month of PSN service," 6 May 2011, accessed 28 September 2014, http://bgr.com/2011/05/06/sonys-ceo-apologizes-for-security-breach-will-offer-free-month-of-psn-service/; [i] Sony Computer Entertainment and Sony Network Entertainment, "Update on PlayStation Network and Qriocity," *PlayStation Blog*, 26 April 2011, accessed 25 September 2014, http://blog.us.playstation.com/2011/04/26/update-on-playstation-network-and-qriocity/; [j] British Broadcasting Corporation, "Sony asks gamers to sign new terms or face PSN ban," *British Broadcasting Corporation*, 16 September 2011, accessed 28 September 2014, http://www.bbc.co.uk/news/technology-14948701; [k] Keith Stuart and Charles Arthur, "PlayStation Network hack: why it took Sony seven days to tell the world," *The Guardian,* 27 April 2011, accessed 27 September 2014, http://www.theguardian.com/technology/gamesblog/2011/apr/27/playstation-network-hack-sony; [l] Sony Online Entertainment, "Sony Online Entertainment Announces Theft of Data from Its Systems," 3 May 2011, accessed 28 September 2014, https://www.soe.com/securityupdate/pressrelease.vm; [m] Jordan Robertson and Ryan Nakashima, "Sony: Credit data risked in PlayStation network outage," *Mass Live,* 28 April 2011, accessed 25 September 2014, http://www.masslive.com/news/index.ssf/2011/04/sony_credit_data_risked_in_pla.html; [n] Semiconportal, "Sony asks FBI to investigate unauthorized network intrusion," 2 May 2011, accessed 28 September 2014, https://www.semiconportal.com/en/archive/news/main-news/110502-sony-network-intrusion.html; [o] Andrew Webster, "FBI investigating PSN hack; Sony looking into compensating users," *Ars Technica*, 29 April 2011, accessed 28 September 2014, http://arstechnica.com/gaming/2011/04/sony-looking-into-compensating-psn-users-fbi-gets-involved/; [p] Larry Dignan, "Sony's data breach costs likely to scream higher," *ZD Net*, 24 May 2011, accessed 27 September 2014, http://www.zdnet.com/blog/btl/sonys-data-breach-costs-likely-to-scream-higher/49161.

Heartland Payment Systems 2008: [q] Brian Krebs, "Hacker Ring Stole 160 Million Credit Cards," 25 July 2013, accessed 29 September 2014, http://krebsonsecurity.com/tag/heartland-payment-systems/; [r] Brian Krebs, "Payment Processor Breach May Be Largest Ever," 20 January 2009, accessed 29 September 2014, http://voices.washingtonpost.com/securityfix/2009/01/payment_processor_breach_may_b.html; [s] Paul J. Fishman, "United States of America v. Vladimir Drinkman, Aleksandr Kalinin, Roman Kotov, Mikhail Rytikov, and Dmitriy Smiliantets," July 2013, 7, accessed 29 September 2014, http://krebsonsecurity.com/wp-content/uploads/2013/07/DVKRK-Indictment.pdf; [t] Brian Prince describes the discovery of the Heartland breach during the week of 12 January 2009 and reported to the public on 20 January 2009. Brian Prince, "Heartland Payment Systems Reports Breach," 20 January 2009, accessed 29 September 2014, http://www.eweek.com/c/a/Security/Heartland-Payment-Systems-Reports-Breach/; [u] Thomas Claburn, "Heartland Payment Systems Hit By Data Security Breach," 20 January 2009, accessed 29 September 2014, http://www.darkreading.com/attacks-and-breaches/heartland-payment-systems-hit-by-data-security-breach/d/d-id/1075770?; [v] Department of Justice, "Alleged International Hacker Indicted for Massive Attack on U.S. Retail and Banking Networks," 17 August 2009, accessed 29 September 2014, http://www.justice.gov/opa/pr/alleged-international-hacker-indicted-massive-attack-us-retail-and-banking-networks; [w] Department of Justice, "Five Indicted in New Jersey for Largest Known Data Breach Conspiracy," 25 July 2013, accessed 29 September 2014, http://www.justice.gov/opa/pr/five-indicted-new-jersey-largest-known-data-breach-conspiracy; [x] Julia S. Cheney, "Heartland Payment Systems: Lessons Learned from a Data Breach," January 2010, 3, accessed 29 September 2014, http://www.phil.frb.org/consumer-credit-and-payments/payment-cards-center/publications/discussion-papers/2010/d-2010-january-heartland-payment-systems.pdf; [y] Robert McMillan, "SEC, FTC Investigating Heartland After Data Theft," 25 February 2009, accessed 30 September 2014, http://www.pcworld.com/article/160264/heartland_investigated_by_sec_ftc.html.

Through the comparison of these three incidents, many commonalities emerge. The incidents show that cyber-attacks are not specific to a certain type of business model, or network design. Each of the companies chose not to encrypt their payment card information, which placed that information at risk once hackers infiltrated the network. Target, Fazio Mechanical, and Heartland Payment Systems were compliant with industry accepted computer security practices, but these practices were insufficient to prevent the attacks. All three of the attacks contained an international aspect that started with a vulnerability in the United States and ended with information transferred to the Ukraine and Russia. These similarities may prove useful to improve security of sensitive information.

The Federal Government's response was consistent. In each of these incidents, the agencies involved displayed conduct more reactive than proactive. The Secret Service, Federal Bureau of Investigation, Department of Justice, and a few other federal offices, exhibited an investigative posture designed to seek out information after the attacks, rather than a proactive posture that could have prevented the crimes. The actions of these federal agencies demonstrate that the United States does not have a single investigative authority to examine cyber-attacks. Instead, the Department of Justice, and the Secret Service each have related, parallel, and probably coordinated, investigations.

Notably lacking is any mention of involvement from the Department of Defense. None of the literature reviewed mentioned any involvement of the National Security Agency, the United States Strategic Command, or the United States Cyber Command. The surveillance capability of the National Security Agency, along with the response capability of United States Cyber Command is an untapped resource for the defense against national cyber-attacks.

Commercial Security Practices

The commercial security practices, as shown by the case studies, were not sufficient to protect Target, Sony, or Heartland Payment Systems. Heartland Payment Systems, Fazio Mechanical, and Target Corporation were all compliant with industry practices during the attacks on their computer systems. Compliance with the standards did not ensure protection of sensitive customer information.

Heartland Payment Systems seems to be the most egregious case of the security standards failing to achieve protection of payment card information. Several security inspections conducted during the time that Heartland's computer systems contained malware (Cheney 2010, 3-7) is proof that the inspections were inadequate. The standards did not determine if the network was capable of protecting customer information. Heartland received Payment Card Industry Data Security Standard certification in April 2008. Hackers breached the network four months earlier (Claburn 2009).

Fazio Mechanical installed antivirus software, which, technically, met the letter of the law for malware detection capability. However, the version of software they chose did not automatically scan electronic mail for malicious programs. The free version of *Malwarebytes Antivirus* required manual user scans to find any infected computers. In Fazio Mechanical's case, the *Citadel* malware intercepted the login credentials to the Target network prior to detection (Krebs 2014c).

Target was much better postured with its network security, but it chose not to use the purchased tools. Installed *Symantec Antivirus* performed its job of scanning computers for malware. However, security staff ignored alerts when *Symantec* discovered malicious software. Similarly, the FireEye network security system found security issues and issued alerts. Target staff also ignored these alerts (U.S. Senate Committee on Commerce, Science, and Transportation 2013). However, since these systems were installed and operational, Target was able to receive certification as Payment Card Industry Data Security Standard compliant in September 2013, two months prior to the attacks (U.S. Senate Committee on Commerce, Science, and Transportation 2013).

Sony demonstrated its own failures. No literature reviewed definitively stated that Sony was compliant with Payment Card Industry Data Security Standards. However, the volume of credit and debit card transactions attributed to Sony indicates that the company likely received security reviews from the payment card industry. Nevertheless, the facts attest that Sony was not always compliant. Sony retained old and outdated customer payment-card information that Payment Card Industry Data Security Standards required to be destroyed (Klemic 2012). The United Kingdom (BBC News 2013), and the United States (Grande 2014), both ruled against Sony with their poor security practices.

As recently as Target in September 2013, the Payment Card Industry Data Security Standards failed to protect sensitive payment card information. Instead, history indicates that the standards are little more than a checklist with no application to actual security of the information considered sensitive.

In addition to security of the computers and network, security of the information itself is a concern. The Payment Card Industry Data Security Standard does not require information to be encrypted either when it is moving through a network, or when it is at rest stored in a computer. Since encryption was not required for payment card information, the companies in the case studies chose not to implement this additional security measure.

Sony (Stuart and Arthur 2011) and Heartland Payment Systems (Claburn 2009) did not encrypt information. Target encrypted the Personally Identification Numbers used for debit cards, but no other information (Harris et al. 2014). Since Target had the capability to encrypt information, the situation suggests that the retail company considered the remaining information less important or less vulnerable. Regardless of the rationale behind leaving payment card and personally identifiable information unencrypted, the result was customer information placed at a higher risk and more easily obtained by hackers.

Analysis demonstrates that the commercial standards are inadequate to protect sensitive payment card information. The standards were not successful in protecting the large-scale breaches at Target, Sony, or Heartland Payment Systems. These standards will need to evolve to keep up with the emerging transnational threat in cyberspace.

International Nature of Attacks

In all three of these cases, international criminal elements used computer systems from several nations. Actors in Russia (Villeneuve 2014) and Ukraine (Riley et al. 2014) removed information from Target's network to three computers in the United States, and one in Brazil (Krebs 2014b), then off to Ukraine and Russia (Riley et al. 2014). Sony's attack involved fifty-nine different nations (Robertson and Nakashima 2011) with the attacked server in the United States (Miller 2011) and the culprits believed to be in Russia and Ukraine (Poulsen 2011). Hackers attacked the Heartland Payment Systems network in the United States and moved information to computers in the United States,

Latvia, The Netherlands, and Ukraine (U.S. Department of Justice 2009). Transnational criminal elements located in Ukraine and Russia form the thread through each of these incidents. An opportunity exists to counter the cyber-crime emanating from these two nations.

Disconnects in Strategy and Policy

Three aspects of federal strategy and policy demonstrate gaps in the protection of United States cyberspace. The current documents lack a unity of effort in a whole-of-government approach, measures to prevent or stop cyber-attacks are reactive in nature, and partnerships to mitigate cyber-attacks are not sufficient to protect payment card information.

Multiple Agencies with Overlapping Responsibilities

United States national level strategies and policies purport to provide a unified approach to protect cyberspace, while at the same time, dividing the domain up in such a way that unity is impossible to achieve. The 2003 *National Strategy to Secure Cyberspace* divided critical infrastructure into fourteen sectors managed by seven different United States Government agencies. Cyberspace crosses over each of these sectors. The *Strategy* does not specifically address payment card information as it crosses into several sectors managed by the Departments of Homeland Security, Treasury, and Energy. The four remaining department may also have a role with payment card information, but the *Strategy* does not provide sufficient details for this aspect of their respective sectors (U.S. President, 16). Similarly, the 2007 *National Strategy for*

Homeland Security maintained a similar division of cyberspace by dividing critical

infrastructure into seventeen sectors (Homeland Security Council 2007, 27-28).

One of the latest of the national level policies is the interim 2010 document, the

National Cyber Incident Response Plan. This document assigns coordination

responsibilities to the Department of Homeland Security with the National Cybersecurity

and Communications Integration Center assigned as the federal coordinating center. The

Incident Plan divides roles and responsibilities into four lanes. The lanes are homeland

security, intelligence, defense, and law enforcement (U.S. Department of Homeland

Security 2010b, 9).

The roles and responsibilities line up with the missions of defending against

cyberterrorism, cyber-warfare, and cyber-crime. The lanes require the Departments of

Homeland Security, Defense, and Justice to assist one another as coordinated by the

National Cybersecurity and Communications Integration Center.

One of the challenges with responding to cyber-attacks is determining which

department is in charge. In the case studies, the Department of Justice, or its subordinate

agency the Federal Bureau of Investigation, along with the Department of Homeland

Security's Secret Service responded to investigate the attacks. Target held a meeting with

personnel from both the Justice Department and the Secret Service (Target Brands Inc.

2014b). Heartland Payment Systems contacted both as well (Claburn 2009). There is no

one department in charge of investigating cyber-attacks. If nation-state actors were

behind any of these attacks, the Department of Defense would have been involved as

well. The actor determines what our actions are today rather than what damage was done.

The lead department is clear once investigators know the actor and intent. The

Department of Homeland security leads cyberterrorism efforts, the Department of Justice leads most cyber-crime investigations, and the Department of Defense leads defense efforts against cyber-warfare.

Reactive Approach

The Federal Government's role in each of these case studies was limited to investigation after the attacks happened, with one exception, Target. Heartland Payment Systems contacted the Department of Justice and the Secret Service requesting their assistance (Claburn 2009). The Federal Bureau of Investigation worked with Sony to investigate the PlayStation breach (Webster 2011). In the case of Target, federal agencies were proactive with notification. The Department of Justice contacted Target and informed them of the breach ten days after the exfiltration of information began (U.S. Senate Committee on Commerce, Science, and Transportation 2013, 1). This was the first time Target was aware of a problem. In each case, the Federal Government's role was to investigate rather than prevent or mitigate the cyber-attacks.

Reliance on the Commercial Sector

The National Infrastructure Protection Plan of 2009 relies on the idea that voluntary partnerships with the private sector are sufficient to protect the United States critical infrastructure (U.S. Department of Homeland Security 2009). These partnerships include the protection of sensitive information, computers, and networks that host the information, and the transport mechanisms that move the information from one commercial entity to another. The repeated attacks by hackers to acquire payment card information as shown in the case studies of Heartland Payment Systems, Sony, and

Target breaches demonstrate that the commercial standards are inadequate. By extension, partnerships between government and those same industries are insufficient to protect sensitive information. Nearly six years after Heartland's breach, Target committed some of the same mistakes, which resulted in similar exfiltration of payment cards. Relying on the commercial sector to self-correct its errors is not sufficient as a national strategy. More action is required to ensure the economy continues to run smoothly.

Summary

Analysis of the Target, Sony, and Heartland Payment Systems case studies show that the United States payment card information is under attack from transnational actors. Criminal actors appear to be behind the three case studies examined. However, terrorist or nation-state actors could just as easily be behind the next set of cyber-attacks. The policies currently employed by the United States have not stopped these attacks, nor have they provided a clear path to defend the nation's economy. The United States can do more to ensure that the American way of life will continue, as the nation remains reliant on our payment card systems and the cyberspace that enable those transactions.

CHAPTER 5

CONCLUSIONS AND RECOMMENDATIONS

That's why, in the years to come, we will have to keep working hard to strike the
appropriate balance between our need for security and preserving those freedoms
that makes us who we are. That means reviewing the authorities of law
enforcement, so we can intercept new types of communication, but also build in
privacy protections to prevent abuse.
— NSA: Missions, Authorities, Oversight and Partnerships, President Obama

Conclusions

The evidence draws several conclusions from the three case studies. First, the

payment card stakeholders have not designed the Payment Card Industry Data Security

Standards adequately to protect sensitive information. Second, with or without these

standards, the federal laws do not adequately address the transnational nature of

cyberspace, or the speed of cyber-attacks on the United States. Finally, the existing

United States response to cyber-attacks is reactive when events occur rather than

proactive to mitigate or prevent widespread damage. For each of these conclusions, the

author recommends courses of action that can mitigate the shortcomings.

Conclusion 1: Payment Card Industry Standards Insufficient

Two of the three incidents described in the case studies showed compliance with

their specific industry standards for computer security. The indications from the four

companies involved show that attacks were not expected. Their actions demonstrate that

security was a much lower priority than required to protect payment card information.

Target received certification in September 2013 as compliant with the Payment

Card Industry Data Security Standards. The standards required network security measures to include firewalls, intrusion detection capabilities, and malware detection software (U.S. Senate Committee on Commerce, Science, and Transportation 2013, 7). The installed *Symantec Antivirus* and FireEye security systems contributed to meeting certification requirements. However, even though these systems existed, they were not utilized effectively which resulted in payment card information theft.

Similar to Target, Heartland Payment Systems received certification in April 2008 stating that they were compliant with Payment Card Industry Data Security Standards (Claburn 2009). Interesting in Heartlands case is that the company received this certification while malware was in the company's network and while hacker had access to their computers (Claburn 2009). The audits and inspections conducted to gain the required certification were insufficient and perhaps even negligent since they failed to uncover the exact activity they should have identified and prevented.

Sony's certification status is not clear. Where Fazio Mechanical (Riley et al. 2014), Target (U.S. Senate Committee on Commerce, Science, and Transportation 2014), and Heartland Payment systems (Claburn 2009) all touted their compliance with industry security practices, Sony remained silent. Regardless, their treatment of old, outdated, and unneeded information shows that they were not compliant with all Payment Card Industry Data Security Standards (Chung 2013).

The industry compliance in these case studies shows that the accepted standards were insufficient to protect the theft of payment card information. Certification of vendors as industry compliant has not protected sensitive information nor has it identified hackers in the network at the time of the inspections. These standards are inadequate for the security tasks they purport to achieve and require additional measures to ensure they can protect payment card information from future attacks.

Conclusion 2: Laws Inadequate to Secure Cyberspace

Existing laws require a determination as to whether a cyber-attack is occurring from the actions of a terrorist organization, criminal element, or nation-state actors. When such a determination is possible, it takes time. While a determination is unknown, it is unclear which department has jurisdiction. Cyberterrorism belongs to the Department of Homeland Security. Transnational cyber-crime belongs to the Federal Bureau of Investigation. Financial crime and identify theft belong to the Secret Service. Cyber-warfare, or cyber-attacks sponsored or controlled by nation-states, belongs to the Department of Defense. These roles and responsibilities are confusing at best since the culprit behind cyberspace activities is not always apparent. The transnational nature of cyberspace also adds to the confusion. The United States requires clearer legal authorities that allow action to move forward regardless of the actor behind the attacks. The laws today confuse who is in charge and delay action to protect the United States.

The National Security Agency has authority to collect information on foreign nationals and organizations outside of the United States. The Agency can also request authorities on certain persons and organizations within the United States, as approved by the Foreign Intelligence Surveillance Court. As it exists today, the *Foreign Intelligence Surveillance Act* does not allow intelligence collection in the United States if it cannot be determined who is behind the attack. In other words, if a nation-state actor or terrorist organization is unconfirmed as behind a cyber-attack, then the Foreign Intelligence Surveillance Court cannot authorize surveillance in the United States.

99

The Target case study shows the problem with this logic. Three computers in the United States were intermediaries to move information from Target's network to a computer in Ukraine. Foreign hackers controlled these computers. If the National Security Agency discovered the payment card information moving to a computer in Ukraine, it could not trace that action back to Target. The Agency would see information moving from three computers in the United States, but could not continue surveillance to determine where that information originated. By stopping short of those three computers in the United States, it is impossible to determine that Target was the victim.

The current laws do not adequately address the transnational nature of cyberspace or the speed that activity can occur. Security of the United States payment card information requires changes to existing law to bridge the roles and responsibilities of federal departments. Security of the nation should not wait for an investigation to determine who is behind a cyber-attack.

Conclusion 3: Proactive Federal Government Approach Required

The Department of Justice, Federal Bureau of Investigation, and the Secret Service are reactive in their approach to network breaches. In the case of Sony (Sherr and Wingfield 2011) and Heartland Payment Systems (Krebs 2009), the victim company notified the law enforcement agencies that a network breach had occurred. Target is the exception.

The Department of Justice contacted Target on 12 December 2013 and requested a meeting to discuss the beach of the retail store's network (U.S. Senate Committee on Commerce, Science, and Transportation 2013, 1). Target held the meeting on 13 December 2013. In attendance were both the Department of Justice and the Secret

Service (Harris et al. 2014). During this meeting, the two government agencies notified Target of the possible intrusion into their network. The Department of Justice demonstrated knowledge of the problem before Target did. This may be due to the Secret Service monitoring the sale of stolen credit card information on the Internet (Riley et al. 2014). Law enforcement's proactive approach to the breach was limited to notifying Target of the problem.

In the Sony and Heartland breaches, law enforcement was limited to reactive approaches of investigating activities after the events took place. The Secret Service confirmed an investigation into the Target breach (Stock 2013). The Federal Bureau of Investigation confirmed an investigation into the Sony breach (Webster 2011). Several federal agencies investigated the Heartland breach (McMillan 2009).

Throughout the three case studies, there was no reported response or reaction from the Department of Defense, the National Security Agency, United States Strategic Command, or United States Cyber Command. The United States Strategic Command, with its cyberspace mission, has the role to "deter and prevent" attacks (U.S. Strategic Command, Public Affairs Office 2014). This proactive approach of the combatant command, and its subordinate command United States Cyber Command, is much different from the reactive approach of law enforcement agencies of both the Department of Justice and the Department of Homeland Security. However, the author found no evidence of a proactive response of the United States Strategic Command, United States Cyber Command, National Security Agency, or any other branch of the Department of Defense.

Moving from a reactive investigative strategy to a proactive protective strategy will allow better protection of sensitive payment card information. Information owners cannot control sensitive data once it leaves a victim network. Proactively seeking out the adversaries actions will allow authorities to shut down the hackers operations prior to them developing into economic disasters for the affected companies, financial organizations, and American citizens. By proactively engaging the adversaries systems, the United States can contain data exfiltration to perhaps tens or hundreds of victim accounts rather than millions of accounts seen today.

Recommendations

The evidence shows that the United States can do more to protect payment card information. The payment card stakeholders can change the Payment Card Industry Data Security Standards to improve the protection of customer information. Congress can amend laws to streamline the government's responses to cyber-attacks to improve unity of effort between agencies and proactively stop the cyber-attacks. The President and Department Secretaries can modify their respective strategy and policy to more proactive approaches to protect cyberspace resources.

Recommendation 1: Improve Commercial Information Security Standards

To protect the United States against future cyber-attacks, the payment card companies must improve the Payment Card Industry Data Security Standards. One element that hackers are doing well, but industry is doing poorly, is functional testing of their security systems. A second is implanting encryption for information in storage as well as information moving throughout a network.

The Payment Card Industry should amend their process and require intrusive tests as part of the certification process. Intrusive testing involves the use of trusted hacker to find weaknesses in the tested network in order to find and fix the vulnerabilities. Adopting this approach may require additional certification for security consulting companies as capable of friendly hacking into commercial networks. Today, some businesses hire 'white-hat' hackers to examine their networks and discover their computer security vulnerabilities. However, the Payment Card Industry does not require this approach. Adding this type of testing will require resources of time and money, but the cost of a breach is much higher than what the intrusive testing will cost.

In addition to intrusive testing, the Payment Card Industry Data Security Standards should adopt data encryption as a requirement. In each of the case studies, hackers were able to benefit from easily read unencrypted information once in the victim network. Encrypted information, however, reduces the value of the information to hackers and improves the defense of the sensitive information. Encryption standards should be required for both stationary information within computer systems as well as moving information through a network. Adoption of encryption will reduce risk significantly.

The commercial sector can benefit greatly from partnership with the Federal Government to protect their critical resources. Law enforcement agencies have a wealth of information that can help bolster systems to protect payment card information. Similarly, the Department of Defense has resources familiar with methods to infiltrate networks. The knowledge of both law enforcement agencies and the Department of Defense can identify and improve network security. A partnership between industry, the

Secret Service, Federal Bureau of Investigation, and the Department of Defense will greatly improve the United States ability to protect against cyber-attacks.

The Secret Service and the Federal Bureau of Investigation have numerous ongoing investigations into cyber-attacks. Some of these attacks successfully penetrated into commercial enterprises. Others security practices protected attacks from gaining access to sensitive information. Information sharing of both successful and unsuccessful security strategies can greatly assist in network security improvements.

The Department of Defense can assist the future improvement of Payment Card Industry Data Security Standards. The National Security Administration and United States Cyber Command have decades of experience with cyber-attacks. Both organizations are aware of threats that exist to attack government networks, as well as hacking abilities of organized crime, terrorists, and nation state actors. Using this wealth of experience, the National Security Administration and the United States Cyber Command can collaborate with industry to co-develop future standards for the civil sector, including encryption standard.

Additionally, as requested by commercial companies, and on a reimbursable basis, the United States Cyber Command can perform intrusive testing on a company's network to determine weaknesses and offer options for consideration to improve security and mitigate any vulnerabilities. To enable this course of action, United States law would need to allow reimbursement to go back to the operations funds of the assisting agency.

Any effort between the Department of Defense and the private sector would benefit greatly by synchronizing the effort through the Department of Homeland Security's National Cybersecurity and Communications Integration Center. The

Memorandum of Agreement Between The Department of Homeland Security and the Department of Defense Regarding Cybersecurity outlines relationships between these federal agencies to build on this type of effort with the civil sector.

Recommendation 2: Revise Federal Laws to Protect Cyberspace

Congress should amend the *Foreign Intelligence Surveillance Act* to reflect the transnational nature of cyber-attacks. The *Act* allows collection activities within the United States, but only if these activities are controlled or sponsored by a foreign government or terrorist organization (U.S. Government 1978). The requirement to determine who is attacking the United States prior to authorizing surveillance is counterproductive to protect the nation. As written today, the law does not consider the nature of cyberspace or the problems of confining cyberterrorism, cyber-crime, and cyber-warfare to specific departments. Congress should amend the law to allow the Foreign Intelligence Surveillance Court to approve surveillance activities when foreign actors or organizations control computers in the United States, regardless of their status as terrorists or nation state actors.

The National Security Agency already has the authorities to monitor information on foreign nationals and systems outside of the country through the authorities of Executive Order 12333 *United States Intelligence Activities*. This authority allows the intelligence community to understand threats to the nation prior to and during attacks. As part of this information collection, connections between people, organizations, and systems are learned. These connections may involve residents, or systems, located in the United States. If the surveillance involves nation-state or terrorist organizations, the Foreign Intelligence Surveillance Court may approve collection activities within the national boundaries. However, a determination that confirms terrorists or nation states is required.

By removing the determination requirement, a continuous surveillance activity provides information to the Departments of Defense, Homeland Security, or Justice, as warranted by the situation. The intent of all of these departments is to protect and defend the United States. Laws that divide these roles into lanes of responsibility can break up an investigation of events and lead to lengthy response times.

Improvements in interagency information sharing can benefit by synchronizing the effort through the Department of Homeland Security's National Cybersecurity and Communications Integration Center and the National Security Agency/Central Security Service Threat Operations Center. The *Memorandum of Agreement Between The Department of Homeland Security and the Department of Defense Regarding Cybersecurity* improved information sharing by connecting the two departments through these operational centers. Incorparation of the Secret Service and the Federal Bureau of Investigation would complete the cyber-centers as a true all-agency cyberspace operations center and allow for full information sharing across the Federal Government.

Recommendation 3: Revise Department of Defense Strategies

Snowden's revelations of National Security Agency functions described a well-developed surveillance and information correlation capability. None of the Snowden documents revealed specific efforts to look for payment card information. However, the same tactics and techniques that the National Security Agency has used to collect metadata from electronic mail (U.S. Office of the Director of Intelligence, 2014) could be modified to monitor for payment card information crossing the Internet.

106

To use the existing National Security Agency's capabilities to protect the United States economy, surveillance activities should seek out credit and debit card information transitioning to international destinations from the United States. Specifically, the Agency should monitor data traveling into Russia and Ukraine looking for large amounts of payment card information. Once discovered, the intelligence community should analyze the flow of data to determine the origin victim. United States citizens and their systems are not the intended targets of this surveillance. Since this recommendation falls within the current roles and responsibilities of the Agency, public and congressional resistance to this mission is not expected. This capability may nest with the previous recommendation to modify the *Foreign Intelligence Surveillance Act,* but those domestic authorities are not necessarily required.

To better define the Department of Defense's role in defending cyberspace, the Secretary should revise the *Strategy for Homeland Defense and Defense Support of Civil Authorities* to include specific actions to defend cyberspace. The current strategy contains two missions. The Secretary should add cyberspace as a third mission with two objectives: Provide intelligence support to law enforcement agencies, and Counter cyberspace threats that put the American way of life in jeopardy. These two objectives show the importance of the cyberspace domain to defending the nation and assist in efforts to aim subordinate policy.

To assist with national goals, the President should amend Executive Order 13636: *Improving Critical Infrastructure Cybersecurity.* The amendment should make a bold statement that America will proactively protect the United States cyberspace infrastructure and the information that it contains by responding to all foreign threats with all instruments of national power, including military force, if needed. The intent of the policy is not to roll tanks into the backyard of a cyber-criminal, but to allow for the use of United Sates Cyber Command to respond, disabling any attacks originating from foreign soil.

Recommendation 4: Merge Federal Cyber-crime Investigative functions

One final recommendation involves law enforcement agencies. The United States should consolidate the cyber investigative functions of the Secret Service into the cyber investigative functions of the Federal Bureau of Investigation. This consolidation effort will merge the thirty-one Electronic Crimes Task Forces of the Secret Service and the National Cyber Investigative Joint Task Force of the Federal Bureau of Investigation into a single organization. Both functions are law enforcement and easily fall within the bounds of the Department of Justice. Requiring two different agencies under two different departments competing for finite resources is not conducive to a United States whole-of-government unified approach. Today, both are involved with on-site visits to victims. In Targets case, both attended a meeting to notify Target of the breach. Both conducted interviews and independent, but likely coordinated investigations. The Federal Bureau of Investigation is responsible for crimes that intrude into computer networks. The Secret Service is responsible for investigating financial related cyber-crime and identity theft. Payment card theft falls within both jurisdictions with no clear leader. Integrating both functions into a single cyber-crime investigative unit will aid victims by providing a single point of contact. It will aid the United States Government by removing the potential for two departments to compete for resources to accomplish the same goals.

It will also allow eliminate redundancy and required coordination by placing the full responsibility with a single agency, the Federal Bureau of Investigation.

To assist law enforcement efforts, Congress should amend United States Code 18 to include cyber incidents as a specific section of concern. Under sections 175, 229E, 831, and 2332, the Department of Justice may request assistance from the Department of Defense to assist with law enforcement efforts to counter biological weapons, chemical weapons, explosives, and weapons of mass destruction, respectively. However, the Department of Defense does not have the authority to assist with cyber-security or searches, and seizures for cybercrime. Congress should amend United States Code 18 to allow the Attorney General to request assistance from the Department of Defense to further law enforcement aims, when needed.

Recommendation for Further Research

This study revealed a lack in adherence to the commercial security practices developed by the retail and maintenance communities. Although there are a number of discrepancies that were identified that are worthy of mention, the extent of adherence to the standards is unknown. A more thorough study could quantify the communities' acceptance of the standards and develop recommendations to make it more acceptable to apply those standards to daily activities. A future author should study the concept of an outside agency, possibly under the Department of Treasury, to determine how to protect the United States economy.

Closing Remarks

The United States relies on cyberspace as a necessary domain that enables Americans' to enjoy life, liberty, and the pursuit of happiness. The economy is a necessary piece of that lifestyle and relies on cyberspace in the form of transmitted financial transactions and payment card information across the Internet. Companies leverage the relatively cheap and easily available Internet to connect their stores, financial institutions, suppliers, and business partners. United States' reliance on cyberspace is one of our greatest enablers of our connected economy, but also one of our greatest vulnerabilities.

The strength of our economy requires a secure and robust cyberspace infrastructure. However, ever-continuing attacks on our sensitive payment card information will likely continue into the future. The commercial standards that protect our personal information are unable to keep pace with the changing tactics and procedures of cyber-attackers. The systems in place are no longer able to protect our personally identifiable and payment card information. Transnational actors continue to find new and improved ways to gain access to our sensitive information. Ignoring the threat will not make it go away. The current policies and procedures are not providing the security required. The United States demands trust in cyberspace to allow the economy to function.

To maintain the American way of life, the national strategy, policy, and laws must keep pace with the changing global landscape. No nation can contain the Internet within their borders. Security rules must recognize the international aspect of our interconnected world. As the Internet continues to grow, so will the threats to our cyberspace systems.

The government owes security to its citizens to allow them to continue to enjoy the freedoms of an open society. That same open and free nature allows hackers to infiltrate private systems with sensitive information. Americans value privacy rights. Strategy, policy, and law must observe those rights while maintaining security.

The Department of Defense has a role and responsibility to defend against all enemies, foreign and domestic. Cyberspace tends to blur some of those lines between what is foreign and what is domestic as external actors continue to use systems within our nation's borders. American laws must evolve to bridge the gap between actors at home and those abroad. Regardless of where an attack comes from, the nation must be ready to defend itself.

GLOSSARY

Critical infrastructure—are "systems and assets, whether physical or virtual, so vital to the United States that the incapacity or destruction of such systems and assets would have a debilitating impact on security, national economic security, national public health or safety, or any combination of those matters" (U.S. President 2013c).

Cyber-crime—is "any illegal activity that uses a computer as its primary means of commission. The U.S. Department of Justice expands the definition of cyber-crime to include any illegal activity that uses a computer for the storage of evidence" (Rouse 2010b).

Cyber infrastructure—"includes electronic information and communication systems, and the information contained in these systems. Computer systems, control systems such as Supervisory Control and Data Acquisition (SCADA) systems, and networks such as the Internet are all part of cyber infrastructure" (U.S. Department of Homeland Security 2009, 12).

Cyberterrorism—"the intimidation of civilian enterprise through the use of high technology to bring about political, religious, or ideological aims actions that result in disabling or deleting critical infrastructure data or information" (Tafoya 2011).

Cyber-warfare—"is any virtual conflict initiated as a politically motivated attack on an enemy's computer and information systems. Waged via the Internet, these attacks disable financial and organizational systems by stealing or altering classified data to undermine networks, websites, and services" (Janssen 2014).

Cyberspace—"is a global domain within the information environment consisting of the interdependent network of information technology infrastructures and resident data, including the Internet, telecommunications networks, computer systems, and embedded processors and controllers" (Joint Chiefs of Staff 2012, II-9).

Cyberspace domain—is a "domain characterized by the use of electronics and the electromagnetic spectrum to store, modify, and exchange data via networks systems and associated physical infrastructures (Joint Chiefs of Staff 2006, ix).

Department of Defense Cyber Crime Center (DC3)—is responsible to deliver "digital forensics and multimedia laboratory services, cyber technical training, and digital forensics research development test and evaluation to a range of [Department of Defense] customers, in addition to cyber analysis for investigative, Information Assurance, and information operations requirements" (U.S. Department of Homeland Security 2009, N-6 - N-7).

Emergency support functions—are "a grouping of government and certain private-sector capabilities into an organizational structure to provide the support, resources, program implantation, and services that are most likely to be needed to save lives, protect property and the environment, restore essential services and critical infrastructure, and help victims and communities return to normal, when feasible, following domestic incidents" (Joint Chiefs of Staff 2013b, GL-6).

Foreign intelligence—"information relating to the capabilities, intentions, or activities of foreign governments or elements thereof, foreign organizations, foreign persons, or international terrorists" (U.S. President 2008b).

Foreign Intelligence Surveillance Act of 1978 (FISA)—"The Foreign Intelligence Surveillance Act of 1978 prescribes procedures for requesting judicial authorization for electronic surveillance and physical search of persons engaged in espionage or international terrorism against the United States on behalf of a foreign power. Requests are adjudicated by a special eleven member court called the Foreign Intelligence Surveillance Court" (Federation of American Scientists 2014).

Foreign Intelligence Surveillance Court (FISC)—"The Foreign Intelligence Surveillance Court was established by Congress in 1978. The Court entertains applications made by the United States Government for approval of electronic surveillance, physical search, and certain other forms of investigative actions for foreign intelligence purposes." (U.S. Foreign Intelligence Surveillance Court 2014b)"Pursuant to FISA, the Court entertains applications submitted by the United States Government for approval of electronic surveillance, physical search, and other investigative actions for foreign intelligence purposes. Most of the Court's work is conducted ex parte as required by statute, and due to the need to protect classified national security information" (U.S. Foreign Intelligence Surveillance Court 2014b).

Hackers—are "individuals or small groups of people (who) can illegally disrupt or gain access to a network or computer system" (U.S. Department of the Air Force 2011).

Homeland—is "the physical region that includes the continental United States, Alaska, Hawaii, United States territories, and surrounding territorial waters and airspace" (Joint Chiefs of Staff 2013b, GL-6).

Homeland defense—is the "protection of United States Sovereignty, territory, domestic population, and critical infrastructure against external threats and aggression or other threats as directed by the President" (Joint Chiefs of Staff 2013a, GL-9).

Homeland security—is a "concerted national effort to prevent terrorist attacks within the United States, reduce America's vulnerability to terrorism, major disasters, and other emergencies; and minimize the damage and recover from attacks, major disasters, and other emergencies that occur" (Joint Chiefs of Staff 2013a, GL-9).

Hostile act—is an "attack or other use of force against the United States, United States forces or other designated persons or property to preclude or impede the mission and/or duties of United States forces, including the recovery of United States personnel or vital United States Government property" (Joint Chiefs of Staff 2013b, GL-6).

Immediate response—is any "form of immediate action taken in the United States and territories to save lives, prevent human suffering, or mitigate great property damage in response to a request for assistance from a civil authority, under imminently serious conditions when time does not permit approval from a higher authority" (Joint Chiefs of Staff 2013b, GL-6).

Incident—is an "occurrence, caused by either human action or natural phenomena, that requires action to prevent or minimize loss of life, or damage, loss of, or other risks to property, information, and/or natural resources" (Joint Chiefs of Staff 2013b, GL-6).

Incident awareness and assessment—is "Secretary of Defense approved use of Department of Defense intelligence, surveillance, reconnaissance, and other intelligence capabilities for domestic non-intelligence support for defense support of civil authorities" (Joint Chiefs of Staff 2013b, GL-7).

International Criminal Police Organization (INTERPOL)—is "the world's largest police organization with 190 member countries. Its primary role is to assist law enforcement agencies around the world in combating all forms of transnational crime and terrorism" (INTERPOL 2014).

Mission assignment—is the "vehicle used by the Department of Homeland Security/Emergency Preparedness and Response/Federal Emergency Management Agency to support federal operations in a Stafford Act major disaster or emergency declaration that orders immediate, short-term emergency response assistance when and applicable state or local government is overwhelmed by the event and lacks the capability to perform, or contract for, the necessary work" (Joint Chiefs of Staff 2013b, GL-7).

National Cyber Investigative Joint Task Force (NCIJTF)—"the multiagency national focal point for coordinating cyber investigations across all national security and criminal law enforcement programs" (U.S. Department of Homeland Security 2010b, 7).

National emergency—is a "condition declared by the President or the Congress by virtue of powers previously vested in them that authorize certain emergency actions to be undertaken in the national interests" (Joint Chiefs of Staff 2013b, GL-7).

National Cybersecurity and Communications Integration Center (NCCIC)— is an operations center that "provides cross-domain situational awareness, including a continuously updated, comprehensive picture of cyber threats, vulnerabilities, and consequences to provide indications and warning of imminent incidents, and to support a coordinated incident response." (U.S. Department of Homeland Security 2010b, 3-4).

National Infrastructure Coordinating Center (NICC)—is "a component of the [Department of Homeland Security National Operations Center], the NICC monitors the Nation's Critical Infrastructure, and Key Resources on an ongoing basis. During an incident, the NICC provides a coordinating forum to share information across Critical Infrastructure and Key Resources sectors through appropriate information sharing entities" (U.S. Department of Homeland Security 2010b, N-3).

National Operations Center (NOC)—"serves as the primary national hub for situational awareness and operations coordination across the Federal Government for incident management. The NOC provides the Secretary of Homeland Security and other principals with information necessary to make critical national-level incident management decisions" (U.S. Department of Homeland Security 2010b, N-3).

Request for assistance—is a "request based on mission requirements and expressed in terms of desired outcome, formally asking the Department of Defense to provide assistance to a local, state, tribal, or other federal agency" (Joint Chiefs of Staff 2013b, GL-8).

Transnational organized crime— is a " self-perpetuating associations of individuals who operate transnationally for the purpose of obtaining power, influence, monetary and/or commercial gains, wholly or in part by illegal means, while protecting their activities through a pattern of corruption and/or violence, or while protecting their illegal activities through a transnational organizational structure and the exploitation of transnational commerce or communication mechanisms" (U.S. President 2011c, i).

APPENDIX A

FEDERAL CYBER INCIDENT LANES

Coordination of Cyber Incident Management			
Coordinating Agency—DHS—responsible for coordinating incident management activities across the breadth of the incident and across all partners. **Coordinating Center—NCCIC**—the point of integration for all information from Federal departments and agencies, State, Local, Tribal, and Territorial Governments, and the private sector related to situational awareness, vulnerabilities, intrusions, incidents, and mitigation activities. **Support to External Stakeholders—NCCIC**—provides multi-directional information sharing across all partners.			
Homeland Security	**Intelligence**	**Defense**	**Law Enforcement**

• **DHS**—works with all partners to establish and maintain Nationally-integrated cybersecurity and communications situational awareness.
 • **DHS**—serves as the National focal point for Cyber Incident management and coordination during cyber-specific incidents.
 Coordinating Centers
 • NCCIC
   - US-CERT
   - NCC
   - ICS-CERT
 • NOC
   - NICC
   - NRCC
 Associated D/As
 • Cabinet departments
 • Independent agencies and government corporations
 Support to External Stakeholders
 • **State, Local, Tribal, and Territorial**—upon request, coordinate and assist with incident response.
 • **Private Sector**—coordinate on the collection, analysis, and sharing of such data in real-time, to help prioritize actions and resource allocation.
	• **IC**—provides attack sensing and warning capabilities to characterize the cyber threat and attribution of attacks and forestall future incidents.
	 Coordination Centers
	 • IC-IRC
	 • NTOC
	 • NCIJTF
	 Associate D/As
	 • Cabinet departments
	 • Independent agencies and government corporations
	 Support to External Stakeholders
	 • **State, Local, Tribal, and Territorial and Private Sector**—share appropriate classified intelligence with cleared CIKR crisis management and threat intelligence groups at the lowest classification possible to allow the provision of sector impact assessment and response coordination.
		• **DOD**—establishes and maintains shared situational awareness and directs the operation and defense of the .mil network.
		 • **DOD**—works with partners to gain attribution of the cyber threat, offer mitigation techniques, and take action to deter or defend against cyber-attacks which pose an imminent threat to national security.
		 • **National Guard Bureau**—communicates and coordinates the synchronization of NG forces (to include but not limited to cyberspace, communications, and signals organizations) in response to cyber incidents
		 Coordinating Centers
		 • JTF-GNO/CYBERCOM
		 • NTOC
		 • DC3
		 Associate D/As
		 • Cabinet departments
		 • Independent agencies and government corporations
		 Support to External Stakeholders
		 State, Local, Tribal, and Territorial—DOD coordinates DSCA when requested
			• **DOJ**—maintains and shares situational awareness about law enforcement activities
			 • **AG**—lead for criminal investigations
			 • **DOJ**—leads the national effort to investigate and prosecute cyber-crime
			 Coordinating Centers
			 • NCIJTF
			 • DC3
			 Associated D/As
			 • FBI
			 • USSS
			 Support to External Stakeholders
			 • **State, Local, Tribal, and Territorial**—DOJ/FBI/NCIJTF coordinates with law enforcement
			 • **Private Sector**—FBI coordinates with InfraGard efforts and works with the private sector regarding the investigation and prosecution of cyber-crime.

Source: Department of Homeland Security, *National Cyber Incident Response Plan: Interim Version, September 2010* (Washington: Department of Homeland Security, 2010), 9.

REFERENCE LIST

Abrams, Rachel. 2014. "Target Puts Data Breach Costs at $148 Million, and Forecasts Profit Drop." *The New York Times*. 5 August. Accessed 24 September 2014. http://www.nytimes.com/2014/08/06/business/target-puts-data-breach-costs-at-148-million.html.

Ackerman, Spencer. 2014. "Utah Lawmaker Floats Bill to Cut Off NSA Data Centre's Water Supply." *The Guardian*. 12 February. Accessed 23 September 2014. http://www.theguardian.com/world/2014/feb/12/utah-lawmaker-nsa-data-centre-water-supply.

Acohido, Byron. 2009. "Hackers Breach Heartland Payment Credit Card Systems." *USA Today*. 23 January. Accessed 24 March 2014. http://usatoday30.usatoday.com/money/perfi/credit/2009-01-20-heartland-credit-card-security-breach_N.htm.

American Civil Liberties Union. 2013. *ACLU vs. James r. Clapper, Keith B. Alexander, Charles T. Hagel, Eric H. Holder, and Robert S. Mueller III.* ACLU v. Clapper - Legal Documents. 11 June. Accessed 7 September 2014. https://www.aclu.org/files/assets/nsa_phone_spying_complaint.pdf.

———. 2014. "ACLU v. Clapper - Challenge to NSA Mass Call-Tracking Program." *Surveillance and Privacy*. Accessed 7 September 2014. https://www.aclu.org/national-security/aclu-v-clapper-challenge-nsa-mass-phone-call-tracking.

Associated Press. 2013. "Verizon Plans Transparency Report on Phone Record Requests, Working with NSA." *Fox News*. 20 December. Accessed 23 September 2014. http://www.foxnews.com/tech/2013/12/20/verizon-plans-transparency-report-phone-requests/.

———. 2014a. "Target Data Breach Cost for Banks Tops $200M." *NBC News*. 18 February. Accessed 25 September 2014. http://www.nbcnews.com/business/business-news/target-data-breach-cost-banks-tops-200m-n33156.

———. 2014b. "Utah Lawmakers Send Mixed Messages to NSA with Measures That Help, Limit Data Center." *Fox News*. 13 February. Accessed 23 September 2014. http://www.foxnews.com/us/2014/02/13/utah-lawmakers-send-mixed-messages-to-nsa-with-measures-that-help-limit-data/.

The Attorney General. 2013. *United States Department of Justice Strategic Plan Fiscal Years 2014-2018*. Accessed 4 September 2014. http://www.justice.gov/jmd/strategic2014-2018/doj-fy-2014-2018-strategic-plan.pdf.

Ax, Joseph. 2014. "U.S. Judge Rules Search Warrants Extend to Overseas Email Accounts." *Reuters*. 25 April. Accessed 30 September 2014.

http://www.reuters.com/article/2014/04/25/us-usa-tech-warrants-idUSBREA3O24P20140425.

Baker, Liana B., and Jim Finkle. 2011. "Sony PlayStation Suffers Massive Data Breach." *Reuters*. 26 April. Accessed 25 September 2014. http://www.reuters.com/article/2011/04/26/us-sony-stoldendata-idUSTRE73P6WB20110426.

Barcy, Jedidiah. 2013. "Tech Firms, Lawmakers Respond to NSA Leak." The Privacy Advisor. 12 June. Accessed 9 September 2014. https://privacyassociation.org/news/a/tech-firms-lawmakers-respond-to-nsa-leak/.

Baxter, Pamela, and Susan Jack. 2008. "Qualitative Case Study Methodology: Study Design and Implementation for Novice Researchers." *The Qualitative Report* 13, no. 4 (4 December): 544-559. Accessed 28 October 2014. http://www.nova.edu/ssss/QR/QR13-4/baxter.pdf.

BBC News. 2011a. "North Korea 'behind South Korean bank cyber hack'." 3 May. Accessed 24 March 2014. http://www.bbc.com/news/world-asia-pacific-13263888.

———. 2011b. "Sony Asks Gamers to Sign New Terms or Face PSN Ban." *BBC*. 16 September. Accessed 28 September 2014. http://www.bbc.co.uk/news/technology-14948701.

———. 2013. "Sony Fined Over 'Preventable' PlayStation Data Hack." *BBC News*. 24 January. Accessed 27 September 2014. http://www.bbc.com/news/technology-21160818.

Berman, Emily. 2011. "Domestic Intelligence: New Powers, New Risks." Brennan Center for Justice. Accessed 22 September 2014. http://www.brennancenter.org/sites/default/files/legacy/AGGReportFINALed.pdf.

Blumenthal, Richard. 2011. "Blumenthal Calls for DOJ Investigation of Sony Playstation Data Breach." Richard Blumenthal United States Senator for Connecticut. 28 April. Accessed 28 September 2014. http://www.blumenthal.senate.gov/newsroom/press/release/blumenthal-calls-for-doj-investigation-of-sony-playstation-data-breach.

Boehning, H. Christopher, and Daniel J. Toal. 2014. "Microsoft Paves the Way for Data Privacy Battle." *The New York Law Journal*. 7 October. Accessed 11 October 2014. http://www.newyorklawjournal.com/id=1202672465322/Microsoft-Paves-the-Way-for-Data-Privacy-Battle?slreturn=20140911211642.

Brandon, John. 2013. "Inside the NSA's secret Utah data center." *Fox News*. 11 June. Accessed 23 September 2014. http://www.foxnews.com/tech/2013/06/11/inside-nsas-secret-utah-data-center/.

Brennan Center for Justice. 2014. "Privacy Board Calls for End to Bulk Collection Program." Brennan Center for Justice. 23 January. Accessed 22 September 2014. http://www.brennancenter.org/press-release/privacy-board-calls-end-bulk-collection-program.

California Legislature. 2014. SB-828 *Assistance to federal agencies.* California Legislative Information. 4 September. Accessed 23 September 2014. http://leginfo.legislature.ca.gov/faces/billCompareClient.xhtml.

California State Senate Rules Committee. 2014. "SB-828 Assistance to federal agencies." Bill Analysis. 19 August. Accessed 23 September 2014. http://leginfo.legislature.ca.gov/faces/billHistoryClient.xhtml#.

Caplin, Nick. 2011. "Some PlayStation Network and Qriocity Services to be Available This Week." *Sony PlayStation Blog.* 1 May. Accessed 28 September 2014. http://blog.eu.playstation.com/2011/05/01/some-playstation-network-and-qriocity-services-to-be-available-this-week/.

Castelli, Christopher J. 2014. "Obama's Top Military Adviser Urges New Federal Cybersecurity Rules." *Inside Cybersecurity.* 8 September. Accessed 23 September 2014. http://insidecybersecurity.com/Cyber-General/Cyber-Public-Content/obamas-top-military-adviser-urges-new-federal-cybersecurity-rules/menu-id-1089.html.

Center for Constitutional Rights. 2013. "Court of Appeals Dismisses CCR Case Challenging NSA Surveillance Program." Center for Constitutional Rights. 20 June. Accessed 22 September 2014. http://ccrjustice.org/newsroom/press-releases/court-of-appeals-dismisses-ccr-case-challenging-nsa-surveillance-program.

———. 2014. "CCR v. Obama (formerly CCR v. Bush)." Center for Constitutional Rights Accessed 22 September 2014. http://ccrjustice.org/CCR-v-Obama.

Chairman of the Joint Chiefs of Staff. 2011. *The National Military Strategy: Redefining America's Military Leadership.* U.S. Department of Defense Publications. 8 February. Accessed 11 October 2014. http://www.army.mil/info/references/docs/NMS%20FEB%202011.pdf.

Cheney, Julia S. 2010. "Heartland Payment Systems: Lessons Learned from a Data Breach." Federal Reserve Bank of Philadelphia. January. Accessed 29 September 2014. http://www.phil.frb.org/consumer-credit-and-payments/payment-cards-center/publications/discussion-papers/2010/d-2010-january-heartland-payment-systems.pdf.

Chung, Emily. 2013. "Sony Data Breach Update Reveals 'Bad Practices'." *CBC News.* 3 May. Accessed 30 September 2014. http://www.cbc.ca/news/technology/sony-data-breach-update-reveals-bad-practices-1.986647.

Claburn, Thomas. 2009. "Heartland Payment Systems Hit By Data Security Breach." *Information Week Dark Reading*. 20 January. Accessed 29 September 2014. http://www.darkreading.com/attacks-and-breaches/heartland-payment-systems-hit-by-data-security-breach/d/d-id/1075770?.

Clapper, James R. 2013. "DNI Statement on Recent Unauthorized Disclosures of Classified Information." *Newsroom*. 6 June. Accessed 31 October 2014. http://www.dni.gov/index.php/newsroom/press-releases/191-press-releases-2013/868-dni-statement-on-recent-unauthorized-disclosures-of-classified-information.

Clarke, Richard A., and Robert K. Knake. 2010. *Cyber War: The Next Threat to National Security and What to Do About It*. New York, NY: HarperCollins e-books, March. http://www.amazon.com/Cyber-War-Threat-National-Security-ebook/dp/B003F1WMAM/ref=sr_1_1?ie=UTF8&qid=1414564391&sr=8-1&keywords=Cyber+War%3A+The+Next+Threat+to+National+Security+and+What+to+Do+About+It

CNN. 2013. "Target: 40 million credit cards compromised." *CNN Money*. 19 December. Accessed 24 September 2014. http://money.cnn.com/2013/12/18/news/companies/target-credit-card/.

———. 2014. "Edward Snowden Fast Facts." *CNN U.S.* 8 February. Accessed 7 September 2014. http://www.cnn.com/2013/09/11/us/edward-snowden-fast-facts/.

Cole, Matthew, and Mike Brunker. 2014. "Edward Snowden: A Timeline." *NBC News*. 25 May. Accessed 7 September 2014. http://www.nbcnews.com/feature/edward-snowden-interview/edward-snowden-timeline-n114871.

Corrin, Amber. 2014. "DoD cyber exercise builds on National Guard's lead." *Federal Times*. 18 July. Accessed 27 September 2014. http://www.federaltimes.com/article/20140718/DHS/307180013/DoD-cyber-exercise-builds-National-Guard-s-lead?odyssey=nav%7Chead.

Credit Finder. 2014. "The PlayStation Hack [Infographic] Are your credit details safe?" Credit Finder. 16 August. Accessed 30 September 2014. http://www.creditcardfinder.com.au/the-sony-playstation-hack-what-it-means-outside-the-gaming-world.html.

Creswell, John W. 2007. *Qualitative Inquiry & Research Design: Choosing Among Five Approaches*. 2nd. ed. Thousand Oaks, CA: Sage Publications.

Daily Mail Reporter. 2011. "'Anonymous' Hackers Hit PlayStation And Sony Websites In Revenge For Lawsuit." *Mail Online*. 6 April. Accessed 27 September 2014. http://www.dailymail.co.uk/sciencetech/article-1373621/Anonymous-hackers-hit-Playstation-Sony-websites-revenge-lawsuit.html?ito=feeds-newsxml.

Dignan, Larry. 2011. "Sony's Data Breach Costs Likely to Scream Higher." *ZDNet*. 24 May. Accessed 27 September 2014. http://www.zdnet.com/blog/btl/sonys-data-breach-costs-likely-to-scream-higher/49161.

Donohue, Laura K. 2013. "NSA Surveillance May Be Legal-But It's Unconstitutional." *Washington Post Opinions*. 21 June. Accessed 7 September 2014. http://www.washingtonpost.com/opinions/nsa-surveillance-may-be-legal--but-its-unconstitutional/2013/06/21/b9ddec20-d44d-11e2-a73e-826d299ff459_story.html.

Elliott, Kennedy, and Terri Rupar. 2013. "Six Months of revelations on NSA." *The Washington Post*. 23 December. Accessed 7 September 2014. http://www.washingtonpost.com/wp-srv/special/national/nsa-timeline/.

Federal Bureau of Investigation. 2014a. *Addressing Threats to the Nation's Cybersecurity*. Accessed 6 June 2014. http://www.fbi.gov/about-us/investigate/cyber/addressing-threats-to-the-nations-cybersecurity-1.

———. 2014b. *The FBI Federal Bureau of Investigation Strategy Map*. Accessed 4 September 2014. http://www.fbi.gov/about-us/strategy-management/fbi-strategy-map.

———. 2014c. *Today's FBI Facts and Figures 2013-2014*. Reports and Publication. Accessed 4 September 2014. http://www.fbi.gov/stats-services/publications/todays-fbi-facts-figures/facts-and-figures-031413.pdf/at_download/file.

———. 2014d. *Quick Facts*. Accessed 4 September 2014. http://www.fbi.gov/about-us/quick-facts.

———. 2014e. *Strategy Management*. The FBI Federal Bureau of Investigation. Accessed 4 September 2014. http://www.fbi.gov/about-us/strategy-management.

Federal Emergency Management Agency. 2013a. *National Level Exercise 2012: Quick Look Report*. Federal Emergency Management Agency. March. Accessed 21 September 2014. http://www.fema.gov/media-library-data/20130726-1911-25045-9856/national_level_exercise_2012_quick_look_report.pdf.

———. 2013b. *The Stafford Act: Robert T. Stafford Disaster Relief and Emergency Assistance Act, as Amended*. April. Accessed 27 May 2014. http://www.fema.gov/media-library-data/1383153669955-21f970b19e8eaa67087b7da9f4af706e/stafford_act_booklet_042213_508e.pdf.

Federation of American Scientists. 2014. *Foreign Intelligence Surveillance Act*. 7 February. Accessed 20 May 2014. http://www.fas.org/irp/agency/doj/fisa/.

Fidel, Raya. 1984. "The Case Study Method: A Case Study." *Library and Information Science Research.* no 6: 273-288. Accessed 28 October 2014. http://faculty.washington.edu/fidelr/RayaPubs/TheCaseStudyMethod.pdf.

Fischer, Eric A. 2013. *Federal Laws Relating to Cybersecurity: Overview and Discussion of Proposed Revisions.* 20 June. Accessed 18 May 2014. http://www.fas.org/sgp/crs/natsec/R42114.pdf.

Fishman, Paul J. 2013. "United States of America v. Vladimir Drinkman, Aleksandr Kalinin, Roman Kotov, Mikhail Rytikov, and Dmitriy Smiliantets ." *Krebs on Security.* July. Accessed 29 September 2014. http://krebsonsecurity.com/wp-content/uploads/2013/07/DVKRK-Indictment.pdf.

Forrester, Anna. 2014. "Cyber Command Leads Exercise to Test Interagency Cybersecurity Coordination; Michael Rogers Comments." *ExecutiveGov.* 18 July. Accessed 17 September 2014. http://www.executivegov.com/2014/07/draft-cyber-command-leads-exercise-to-test-interagency-cybersecurity-coordination-michael-rogers-comments/.

Francis IV, James C. 2014. "13 Mag. 2814 Memorandum and Order." *The American Lawyer.* 25 April. Accessed 30 September 2014. http://pdfserver.amlaw.com/nlj/microsoft-warrant-sdny.pdf.

Gagliordi, Natalie. 2014. "Target's data breach tab: $110 million." *ZDNet.* 5 August. Accessed 24 September 2014. http://www.zdnet.com/target-lowers-quarterly-outlook-due-to-data-breach-costs-7000032336/.

Galante, Joseph, Olga Kharif, and Pavel Alpeyev. 2011. "Sony Network Breach Shows Amazon Cloud's Appeal for Hackers." *Bloomberg.* 16 May. Accessed 30 September 2014. http://www.bloomberg.com/news/2011-05-15/sony-attack-shows-amazon-s-cloud-service-lures-hackers-at-pennies-an-hour.html.

Gellman, Barton. 2013. "NSA broke privacy rules thousands of times per year, audit finds." *The Washington Post.* 15 April. Accessed 23 September 2014. http://www.washingtonpost.com/world/national-security/nsa-broke-privacy-rules-thousands-of-times-per-year-audit-finds/2013/08/15/3310e554-05ca-11e3-a07f-49ddc7417125_story.html.

Gibbs, Samuel. 2014. "US court forces Microsoft to hand over personal data from Irish server." *The Guardian.* 29 April. Accessed 30 September 2014. http://www.theguardian.com/technology/2014/apr/29/us-court-microsoft-personal-data-emails-irish-server.

Goldsmith, Jack L. III. 2004. "Review of the Legality of the STELLAR WIND Program (REDACTED)." American Civil Liberties Union. 6 May. Accessed 10 September 2014. https://www.aclu.org/sites/default/files/assets/olc_stellar_wind_memo_-_may_2004.pdf.

Grande, Allison. 2014. "Sony Gets Nod for $15M Data Breach MDL Settlement." *Law360.* 11 July. Accessed 27 September 2014. http://www.law360.com/articles/556813/sony-gets-nod-for-15m-data-breach-mdl-settlement.

Greenwald, Glenn. 2013. "NSA collecting phone records of millions of Verizon customers daily." *The Guardian.* 5 June. Accessed 7 September 2014. http://www.theguardian.com/world/2013/jun/06/nsa-phone-records-verizon-court-order.

Harris, Davin. 2014. *Surveillance State Exposed: Edward Snowden and the NSA Surveillance Scandal.* Seattle, WA: Amazon Digital Services, 26 January 2014. http://www.amazon.com/Surveillance-State-Exposed-Snowden-Scandal-ebook/dp/B00I2U407O/ref=sr_1_1?ie=UTF8&qid=1414564298&sr=8-1&keywords=Surveillance+State+Exposed#reader_B00I2U407O

Harris, Elizabeth A., Nicole Perlroth, Nathaniel Popper, and Hilary Stout. 2014. "A Sneaky Path into Target Customers' Wallets." *The New York Times.* 18 January. Accessed 24 September 2014. http://www.nytimes.com/2014/01/18/business/a-sneaky-path-into-target-customers-wallets.html.

Haselton, Todd. 2011. "Sony's CEO apologizes for security breach, will offer free month of PSN service." *Boy Genius Report.* 6 May. Accessed 28 September 2014. http://bgr.com/2011/05/06/sonys-ceo-apologizes-for-security-breach-will-offer-free-month-of-psn-service/.

Hatch, David A. 2003. *Cryptologic Almanac 50th Anniversary Series: The Central Security Service.* 28 February. Accessed 8 September 2014. https://www.nsa.gov/public_info/_files/crypto_almanac_50th/The_CSS.pdf.

Hirai, Kazuo, Shinji Hasejima, and Shiro Kambe. 2011. "PlayStation Network / Qriocity: Reportings on illegal and unauthorized intrusion." *Sony.* 1 May. Accessed 28 September 2014. http://www.irwebcasting.com/110501/02/3a33cc2c90/.

Homeland Security Council. 2007. *National Strategy for Homeland Security.* 5 October. Accessed 27 May 2014. http://www.dhs.gov/xlibrary/assets/nat_strat_homelandsecurity_2007.pdf.

INTERPOL. 2014. *General Information about INTERPOL.* Accessed 11 October 2014. http://www.interpol.int/FAQs.

Janssen, Cory. 2014. "Cyberwarafare" *Techopedia.* Accessed 6 June 2014. http://www.techopedia.com/definition/13600/cyberwarfare.

Joint Chiefs of Staff. 2006. *The National Military Strategy for Cyberspace Operations* (redacted and declassified version). Accessed 29 May 2014. http://www.dod.mil/pubs/foi/joint_staff/jointStaff_jointOperations/07-F-2105doc1.pdf.

———. 2012. Joint Publication 3-13, *Information Operations*. 27 November. Accessed 19 May 2014. http://www.dtic.mil/doctrine/new_pubs/jp3_13.pdf.

———. 2013a. Joint Publication 3-27, *Homeland Defense*. 29 July. Accessed 27 May 2014. http://www.dtic.mil/doctrine/new_pubs/jp3_27.pdf.

———. 2013b. Joint Publication 3-28, *Defense Support of Civil Authorities*. 31 July. Accessed 27 May 2014. http://www.dtic.mil/doctrine/new_pubs/jp3_28.pdf.

Kamara, Seny. 2014a. "Restructuring the NSA Metadata Program." Microsoft Research. Accessed 23 September 2014. http://research.microsoft.com/en-us/um/people/senyk/slides/metacrypt.pdf.

———. 2014b. "Seny Kamara." Microsoft Research. Accessed 23 September 2014. http://research.microsoft.com/en-us/um/people/senyk/.

Kaufman, Brett Max. 2013. "A Guide to What We Now Know about the NSA's Dragnet Searches of Your Communications." *Free Future: Protecting Civil Liberties in the Digital Age*. 8 September. Accessed 7 September 2014. https://www.aclu.org/blog/national-security/guide-what-we-now-know-about-nsas-dragnet-searches-your-communications.

Kerner, Sean Michael. 2011. "Deciphering the Sony PSN Attack." *eSecurity Planet*. 2 June. Accessed 28 September 2014. http://www.esecurityplanet.com/trends/article.php/3935046/Deciphering-the-Sony-PSN-Attack.htm.

Kill, Kristin. 2011. "News: Playstation Network Mysteriously 'Down for Maintenance' on 4Chan Attack Day." *The Co-operatives*. 4 April. Accessed 28 September 2014. http://theco-operatives.com/news-playstation-network-mysteriously-down-for-maintenance-on-4chan-attack-day/.

King, Rachael. 2009. "Lessons from the Data Breach at Heartland." *Boomberg Businessweek*. 6 July. Accessed 9 September 2014. http://www.businessweek.com/stories/2009-07-06/lessons-from-the-data-breach-at-heartlandbusinessweek-business-news-stock-market-and-financial-advice.

Kitten, Tracy. 2013a. "Card Fraud Scheme: The Breached Victims." Bank Info Security. 25 July. Accessed 29 September 2014. http://www.bankinfosecurity.com/card-fraud-scheme-breached-victims-a-5941.

———. 2013b. "New Details on Global, Heartland Breaches." Bank Info Security. 29 July. Accessed 24 March 2014. http://www.bankinfosecurity.com/card-fraud-case-sheds-light-on-breaches-a-5946.

Klemic, Kane. 2012. "Payment Card Industry Standards and the Sony Data Breach." *Making a Difference*. 18 September. Accessed 30 September 2014.

http://www.armaedfoundation.org/pdfs/Klemic_Payment_Card_industry_2012.
pdf.

Krebs, Brian. 2009. "Payment Processor Breach May Be Largest Ever." *The Washington Post.* 20 January. Accessed 29 September 2014. http://voices.washingtonpost.com/securityfix/2009/01/payment_processor_breach_may_b.html.

———. 2013a. "Hacker Ring Stole 160 Million Credit Cards." *Krebs on Security.* 25 July. Accessed 29 September 2014. http://krebsonsecurity.com/tag/heartland-payment-systems/.

———. 2013b. "Sources: Target Investigating Data Breach." *Krebs on Security.* 18 December. Accessed 24 September 2014. http://krebsonsecurity.com/2013/12/sources-target-investigating-data-breach/.

———. 2014a. "A First Look at the Target Intrusion, Malware." *Krebs on Security.* 15 January. Accessed 24 September 2014. http://krebsonsecurity.com/2014/01/a-first-look-at-the-target-intrusion-malware/.

———. 2014b. "Target Hackers Broke in Via HVAC Company." *Krebs on Security.* 5 February. Accessed 25 September 2014. http://krebsonsecurity.com/2014/02/target-hackers-broke-in-via-hvac-company/.

———. 2014c. "Email Attack on Vendor Set Up Breach at Target." *Krebs on Security.* 12 February. Accessed 24 September 2014. http://krebsonsecurity.com/2014/02/email-attack-on-vendor-set-up-breach-at-target/.

———. 2014d. "The Target Breach, By the Numbers." *Krebs on Security.* 6 May. Accessed 25 September 2014. http://krebsonsecurity.com/2014/05/the-target-breach-by-the-numbers/.

Levi, Edward H. 2014. "The NSA's Telephone Metadata Program is Unconstitutional." *The BLOG.* 9 January. Accessed 7 September 2014. http://www.huffingtonpost.com/geoffrey-r-stone/the-nsas-telephone-meta-d_b_4571523.html.

Lichtenfels, Rick. 2012. "U.S. Department of Homeland Security's National Cybersecurity and Communications Integration Center." *Cybersecurity Nexus.* 30 April. Accessed 3 September 2014. https://www.isaca.org/chapters2/New-York-Metropolitan/membership/Documents/2012-04-30%20Spring%20Conference-Meeting/2%20Lichtenfels%20DHS%20NCCIC%202.pdf.

Lien, Tracey. 2014. "Sony Agrees to $14M Settlement in 2011 Data Breach Class Action [update]." *Polygon.* 23 July. Accessed 27 September 2014. http://www.polygon.com/2014/7/23/5931793/sony-2011-data-breach-class-action-lawsuit.

Malwarebytes Corporation. 2014. "Malwarebytes Anti-Maleware: The world's most popular anti-malware." Accessed 4 October 2014. https://www.malwarebytes.org/antimalware/.

Martinez, Edecio. 2011. "PlayStation Network breach has cost Sony $171 million." *CBS News.* 24 May. Accessed 5 October 2014. http://www.cbsnews.com/news/playstation-network-breach-has-cost-sony-171-million/.

McConnell, J. M. 2007. *The National Counterintelligence Strategy of the United States of America.* Accessed 23 March 2014. http://www.ncix.gov/publications/strategy/docs/CIStrategy.pdf.

McGlasson, Linda. 2010. "Heartland Hacker Sentenced to 20 Years." *Bank Info Security.* 26 March. Accessed 23 March 2014. http://www.bankinfosecurity.com/heartland-hacker-sentenced-to-20-years-a-2344.

McIntyre, T J. 2014. "United States v. Microsoft (and Ireland)." *IT Law in Ireland.* 16 September. Accessed 30 September 2014. http://www.tjmcintyre.com/2014/09/united-states-v-microsoft-and-ireland.html.

McMillan, Robert. 2009. "SEC, FTC Investigating Heartland After Data Theft." *PC World.* 25 February. Accessed 30 September 2014. http://www.pcworld.com/article/160264/heartland_investigated_by_sec_ftc.html.

Mears, Bill, and Evan Perez. 2013. "Judge: NSA domestic phone data-mining unconstitutional." *CNN Justice.* 16 December. Accessed 7 September 2014. http://www.cnn.com/2013/12/16/justice/nsa-surveillance-court-ruling/.

Messmer, Ellen. 2009. "Debit-card processor claims data breach part of bigger fraud." *Computerworld.* 20 January. Accessed 29 September 2014. http://www.computerworld.com/article/2530570/security0/debit-card-processor-claims-data-breach-part-of-bigger-fraud.html.

Microsoft Corporation. 2013. "Statement of Microsoft Corporation on Customer Privacy." *Microsoft News Center.* 6 June. Accessed 23 September 2014. http://www.microsoft.com/en-us/news/press/2013/jun13/06-06statement.aspx.

Miller, Rich. 2011. "Sony to Reboot Playstation PSN in New Data Center." *Data Center Knowledge.* 2 May. Accessed 28 September 2014. http://www.datacenterknowledge.com/archives/2011/05/02/sony-to-reboot-playstation-psn-in-new-data-center/.

Mogg, Trevor. 2014. "Yahoo Says It Faced $250,000-a-Day Fine for Opposing NSA Data Demand." *Fox News.* 12 September. Accessed 23 September 2014. http://www.foxnews.com/tech/2014/09/12/yahoo-says-it-faced-250000-day-govt-fine-for-opposing-nsa-data-demand/.

Moss, Sebastian. 2013. "Sony Settles Class Action Lawsuit: Over $1 million in Free Games, Themes and PS+ Discounts Available for Canadians." *PlayStation Life Style*. 18 April. Accessed 28 September 2014. http://www.playstationlifestyle.net/ 2013/04/18/sony-settles-class-action-lawsuit-over-1-million-in-free-games-themes-and-ps-discounts-available-for-canadians/.

Napolitano, Janet, and Robert Gates. 2010. *Memorandum of Agreement between the Department of Homeland Security and the Department of Defense Regarding Cybersecurity*. 27 September. Accessed 21 September 2014. http://www.dhs.gov/ xlibrary/assets/20101013-dod-dhs-cyber-moa.pdf.

The National Archives. 2014. *The Charters of Freedom: A New World is at Hand*. Accessed 22 September 2014. http://www.archives.gov/exhibits/charters/ bill_of_rights_transcript.html.

National Institute of Standards and Technology. 2014. *Cybersecurity Framework*. 12 February. Accessed 20 September 2014. http://www.nist.gov/cyberframework/.

National Security Agency. 2010. "NSA/CSS Strategy." June. Accessed 3 September 2014. https://www.nsa.gov/about/_files/nsacss_strategy.pdf.

———. 2013. "The National Security Agency: Missions, Authorities, Oversight and Partnerships." Statements, Speeches, and Testimonies. 9 August. Accessed 7 September 2014. https://www.nsa.gov/public_info/_files/speeches_testimonies/ 2013_08_09_the_nsa_story.pdf.

New Hampshire Department of Safety. 2013. "National Incident Management System Frequency Asked Questions." *NIMS on-line*. May. Accessed 15 September 2014. https://www.nh.gov/safety/divisions/hsem/documents/NIMSQA1305.pdf.

O' Harrow Jr., Robert, and The Washington Post. 2014. *Zero Day: The Threat in Cyberspace*. New York, NY: Diversion Books. 9 January. http://www.amazon.com/Zero-Day-Cyberspace-Washington-Post-ebook/dp/B00B05MQGU/ref=sr_1_1?ie=UTF8&qid=1414564560&sr=8-1&keywords=Zero+Day%3A+The+Threat.

Office of the Assistant Attorney General. 2004. *Memorandum for the Attorney General: Review of the Legality of the STELLAR WIND Program* (declassified and redacted version). 6 May. Accessed 6 September 2014. https://www.aclu.org/sites/default/ files/assets/olc_stellar_wind_memo_-_may_2004.pdf.

Pellerin, Cheryl. 2013. "Cybercom Builds Teams for Offense, Defense in Cyberspace." *DoD News*. 12 March. Accessed 9 September 2014. http://www.defense.gov/ news/newsarticle.aspx?id=119506.

———. 2014. "Rogers: Cybercom Defending Networks, Nation." *DoD News*. 18 August. Accessed 9 September 2014. http://www.defense.gov/news/newsarticle.aspx?id=122949.

Poulsen, Kevin. 2011. "PlayStation Network Hack: Who Did It?" *Wired*. 27 April. Accessed 27 September 2014, http://www.wired.com/2011/04/playstation_hack/.

Prince, Brian 2009a. "Heartland Payment Systems Reports Breach." *eWeek*. 20 January. Accessed 29 September 2014. http://www.eweek.com/c/a/Security/Heartland-Payment-Systems-Reports-Breach/.

———. 2009b. "Details of Heartland, Hannaford Data Breaches Emerge." *eWeek*. 18 August. Accessed 29 September 2014. http://www.eweek.com/c/a/Security/Details-of-Heartland-Hannaford-Data-Breaches-Emerge-788029/.

Privacy and Civil Liberties Oversight Board 2014a. *Report on the Telephone Records Program Conducted under Section 215 of the USA PATRIOT Act and on the Operations of the Foreign Intelligence Surveillance Court*. 23 January. Accessed 23 September 2014. http://www.pclob.gov/Library/215-Report_on_the_Telephone_Records_Program.pdf.

———. 2014b. *Report on the Surveillance Program Operated Pursuant to Section 702 of the Foreign Intelligence Surveillance Act*. 2 July. Accessed 22 September 2014http://www.pclob.gov/Library/702-Report.pdf.

———.2014c. *About the Board*. Accessed 23 September 2014. http://www.pclob.gov/about-us.

Raff, Aviv. 2014. "PoS Malware Targeted Target." *Seculert*. 16 January. Accessed 24 September 2014. http://www.seculert.com/blog/2014/01/pos-malware-targeted-target.html.

Reeves, Ben. 2011. "[UPDATE] Sony Confirms Thousands of Credit Cards Stolen During Hack." *Game Informer*. 2 May. Accessed 28 September 2014. http://www.gameinformer.com/b/news/archive/2011/05/02/thousands-of-credit-cards-stolen-during-second-sony-hack.aspx.

Reisinger, Don. 2011a. "PS3 jailbreak prompts restraining order from Sony." *CNET*. 12 January. Accessed 27 September 2014. http://www.cnet.com/news/ps3-jailbreak-prompts-restraining-order-from-sony/.

———. 2011b. "Geohot starts blog, raises cash for legal fees." *CNET*. 22 February. Accessed 27 September 2014. http://www.cnet.com/news/geohot-starts-blog-raises-cash-for-legal-fees/.

Riley, Michael, Ben Elgin, Dune Lawrence, and Carol Matlack. 2014. "Missed Alarms and 40 Million Stolen Credit Card Numbers: How Target Blew It." *Businessweek.* 13 March. Accessed 14 March 2014. http://www.businessweek.com/articles/ 2014-03-13/target-missed-alarms-in-epic-hack-of-credit-card-data.

Roberts, Marc K. 2014. H.B. 161 *Prohibition on Electronic Data Collection Assistance.* 24 February. Accessed 23 September 2014. http://le.utah.gov/~2014/bills/static/ HB0161.html.

Robertson, Jordan, and Ryan Nakashima. 2011. "Sony: Credit data risked in PlayStation network outage." *Mass Live.* 28 April. Accessed 25 September 2014. http://www.masslive.com/news/index.ssf/2011/04/sony_credit_data_risked_in_pl a.html.

Rose, Mike. 2011. "Canadian Law Firm Files $1B Lawsuit against Sony over PSN Data Breach." *Gamasutra.* 4 May. Accessed 28 September 2014. http://www.gamasutra.com/view/news/34499/Canadian_Law_Firm_Files_1_Billi on_Class_Action_Lawsuit_Against_Sony_Over_PSN_Data_Breach.php.

Roulo, Claudette. 2014. "Alexander: Laws, Policies Lag Behind Changed in Cyber Threats." *DoD News.* 27 February. Accessed 28 May 2014. http://www.defense.gov/news/newsarticle.aspx?id=121745

Rouse, Margaret. 2010a. "HSPD-7 (Homeland Security Presidential Directive No. 7)." *TechTarget.* April. Accessed 19 September 2014. http://searchsecurity. techtarget.com/definition/HSPD-7.

———. 2010b. "Definition: Cybercrime." *TechTarget.* October. Accessed 6 June 2014. http://searchsecurity.techtarget.com/definition/cybercrime.

S, Ben. 2011. "46 DC EA D3 17 FE 45 D8 09 23 EB 97 E4 95 64 10 D4 CD B2 C2." *Yale Law and Technology.* 1 March. Accessed 27 September 2014. http://www.yalelawtech.org/trusted-computing-drm/46-dc-ea-d3-17-fe-45-d8-09- 23-eb-97-e4-95-64-10-d4-cd-b2-c2/

Sang-Hun, Choe. 2013. "Computer Networks in South Korea Are Paralyzed in Cyberattacks." *The New York Times.* 20 March. Accessed 29 October 2014. http://www.nytimes.com/2013/03/21/world/asia/south-korea-computer-network- crashes.html?pagewanted=all&_r=0.

Savage, Charlie. 2014. "U.S. Memo Redactions Leave Doubts on Stellar Wind data Surveillance Program." *The New York Times.* 6 September. Accessed 9 November 2014. http://www.sott.net/article/285367-US-memo-redactions-leave-doubts-on- Stellar-Wind-data-surveillance-program.

Schaaff, Tim. 2011. *Opening Statement of Tim Schaaff, President of Sony Network Entertainment International Before the Subcommittee on Commerce, Manufacturing and Trade of the U.S. House of Representatives Committee on Energy and Commerce.* 2 June. Accessed 27 September 2014. http://democrats.energycommerce.house.gov/sites/default/files/documents/Testimony-Schaaff-CMT-Sony-Epsilon-Data-Security-Legislation-2011-6-2.pdf.

Semiconportal. 2011. "Sony Asks FBI to Investigate Unauthorized Network Intrusion." *Semiconportal.* 2 May. Accessed 28 September 2014. https://www.semiconportal.com/en/archive/news/main-news/110502-sony-network-intrusion.html.

Serabian, John A. Jr. 2000. "Cyber Threats and the US Economy." *News & Information.* 23 February. Accessed 6 June 2014. https://www.cia.gov/news-information/speeches-testimony/2000/cyberthreats_022300.html.

Sethi, Arjun. 2014. "A chance to limit spying on Americans." *CNN Opinion.* 15 August. Accessed 23 September 2014. http://www.cnn.com/2014/08/15/opinion/sethi-nsa-surveillance-bill-americans/index.html?iref=allsearch.

Sherr, Ian, and Nick Wingfield. 2011. "Play by Play: Sony's Struggles on Breach." The *Wall Street Journal.* 7 May. Accessed 25 September 2014. http://online.wsj.com/news/articles/SB10001424052748704810504576307322759299038.

Sony Computer Entertainment and Sony Network Entertainment. 2011. "Update on PlayStation Network and Qriocity." *PlayStation Blog.* 26 April. Accessed 25 September 2014. http://blog.us.playstation.com/2011/04/26/update-on-playstation-network-and-qriocity/.

Sony Online Entertainment. 2011. "Sony Online Entertainment Announces Theft of Data from Its Systems." *Press Release.* 3 May. Accessed 28 September 2014. https://www.soe.com/securityupdate/pressrelease.vm.

State of Utah House Revenue and Taxation Standing Committee. 2014. *Minutes of the House Revenue and Taxation Standing Committee.* 7 March. Accessed 23 September 2014. http://le.utah.gov/~2014/minutes/HREV0307.pdf.

Sternstein, Aliya. 2014. "National Guard, Feds Double Down for Foreign Hacks against Us." *Nextgov.* 17 July. Accessed 17 September 2014. http://www.nextgov.com/cybersecurity/2014/07/national-guard-feds-double-down-foreign-hack-against-us/88987/.

Stock, Kyle. 2013. "Huge Credit Card Heist Puts Target in Legal Crosshairs." *Bloomberg Businessweek.* 19 December. Accessed 24 September 2014. http://www.businessweek.com/articles/2013-12-19/huge-credit-card-heist-puts-target-in-legal-crosshairs.

Stuart, Keith, and Charles Arthur. 2011. "PlayStation Network hack: Why It Took Sony Seven Days To Tell The World." *The Guardian.* 27 April. Accessed 27 September 2014. http://www.theguardian.com/technology/gamesblog/2011/apr/27/playstation-network-hack-sony.

Sudworth, John. 2009. "New 'Cyber Attacks' Hit S Korea." *BBC News.* 9 July. Accessed 24 March 2014. http://news.bbc.co.uk/2/hi/asia-pacific/8142282.stm.

Szoldra, Paul. 2014. "SNOWDEN: Here's Everything We've Learned In One Year Of Unprecedented Top-Secret Leaks." *Business Insider.* 7 June. Accessed 22 June 2014. http://www.businessinsider.com/snowden-leaks-timeline-2014-6.

Tafoya, William L. 2011. "Cyber Terror." *FBI Law Enforcement Bulletin.* November. Accessed 6 June 2014. http://www.fbi.gov/stats-services/publications/law-enforcement-bulletin/november-2011/cyber-terror.

Target Brands Inc. 2014a. "An Update on Our Data Breach and Financial Performance." About Target. 10 January. Accessed 24 September 2014. *Discover.* https://corporate.target.com/discover/article/an-update-on-our-data-breach-and-financial-perform.

———. 2014b. "Data Breach FAQ." Shopping Experience. Accessed 24 September 2014. https://corporate.target.com/about/shopping-experience/payment-card-issue-FAQ.aspx#q6270.

Timberg, Craig. 2013. "NSA Slide Shows Surveillance of Undersea Cables." *The Washington Post.* 10 July. Accessed 7 September 2014. http://www.washingtonpost.com/business/economy/the-nsa-slide-you-havent-seen/2013/07/10/32801426-e8e6-11e2-aa9f-c03a72e2d342_story.html.

Timberg, Craig, and Ellen Nakashima. 2013. "Agreements with Private Companies Protect U.S. Access to Cables' Data for Surveillance." *The Washington Post.* 6 July. Accessed 7 September 2014. http://www.washingtonpost.com/business/technology/agreements-with-private-companies-protect-us-access-to-cables-data-for-surveillance/2013/07/06/aa5d017a-df77-11e2-b2d4-ea6d8f477a01_story.html.

Tirrell, William K. 2012. "American Cybersecurity: Properly Postured in Post 9/11 Security Environment?" Master's thesis, Army Command and General Staff College, 14 December. Accessed 28 May 2014. http://cgsc.cdmhost.com/utils/getdownloaditem/collection/p4013coll2/id/2958/filename/3009.pdf/mapsto/pdf.

United Nations Interregional Crime and Justice Research Institute. 2014. *Issues and Explanations: Cyberwarfare.* Accessed 6 June 2014. http://www.unicri.it/special_topics/securing_cyberspace/cyber_threats/explanations/.

U.S. Army. Command and General Staff College. 2014. ST 20-10, *Master of Military Art and Science (MMAS) Research and Thesis.* Ft. Leavenworth, KS: Government Printing Office, February.

U.S. Cyber Command News Release. 2014. "Cyber Guard Exercise Tests People, Partnerships." *DoD News.* 14 July. Accessed 17 September 2014. http://www.defense.gov/news/newsarticle.aspx?id=122696.

U.S. Cyber Command Public Affairs. 2013. "U.S. Cyber Command." *U.S. Strategic Command Factsheets.* August. Accessed 9 September 2014. http://www.stratcom.mil/factsheets/2/Cyber_Command/.

U.S. Defense Intelligence Agency. 2013. DoD *Information Review Task Force-2 Initial Assessment: Impacts Resulting from the Compromise of Classified Material by a Former NSA Contractor* (redacted and declassified version). 18 December. Accessed 1 November 2014. http://www.dni.gov/files/documents/DOD%20IRTF-2%20Initial%20Assessment.pdf.

U.S. Department of Defense. 2011. *Department of Defense Strategy for Operating in Cyberspace.* July. Accessed 20 September 2014). http://www.defense.gov/news/d20110714cyber.pdf.

———. 2014. "Operations, Series 3-0 Publications, PDFs." *Joint Electronic Library.* 5 August. Accessed 8 September 2014. http://www.dtic.mil/doctrine/new_pubs/jointpub_operations.htm.

U.S. Department of Homeland Security. 2004a. *National Response Framework: Cyber Incident Annex Abstract.* Lessons Learned Information Sharing. 1 December. Accessed 21 September 2014. https://www.llis.dhs.gov/content/national-response-framework-cyber-incident-annex-0.

———. 2004b. *Cyber Incident Annex.* Lessons Learned Information Sharing. December. Accessed 21 September 2014. https://www.llis.dhs.gov/sites/default/files/nrp_cyberincidentannex.pdf.

———. 2006. *Quick Reference Guide for the National Response Plan.* Federal Emergency Management Agency. 22 May. Accessed 15 September 2014. http://www.training.fema.gov/emiweb/downloads/Quick%20Reference%20Guide.pdf.

———. 2008a. *National Response Framework.* Federal Emergency Management Agency. January. Accessed 15 September 2014. http://www.fema.gov/pdf/emergency/nrf/nrf-core.pdf.

———. 2008b. *National Incident Management System*. Federal Emergency Management Agency. 18 December. Accessed 15 September 2014. http://www.fema.gov/pdf/ emergency/nims/NIMS_core.pdf.

———. 2009. *National Infrastructure Protection Plan: Partnering to Enhance Protection and Resiliency*. Accessed 28 May 2014. http://www.dhs.gov/xlibrary/ assets/NIPP_Plan.pdf.

———. 2010a. "*Quadrennial Homeland Security Review Report: A Strategic Framework for a Secure Homeland*. February. Accessed 27 May 2014. http://www.dhs.gov/xlibrary/assets/qhsr_report.pdf.

———. 2010b. *National Cyber Incident Response Plan: Interim Version*. September. Accessed 21 September 2014. http://www.federalnewsradio.com/pdfs/NCIRP_ Interim_Version_September_2010.pdf.

———. 2013a. *National Response Framework Second Edition*. Federal Emergency Management Agency. May. Accessed 3 September 2014. http://www.fema.gov/ media-library-data/20130726-1914-25045-1246/final_national_response_ framework_20130501.pdf.

———. 2013b. *Incentives Study Analytic Report: Executive Order 13636 Improving Critical Infrastructure Cybersecurity*. 12 June. Accessed 20 September 2014. http://www.dhs.gov/sites/default/files/publications/dhs-eo13636-analytic-report-cybersecurity-incentives-study.pdf.

———. 2014a. "National Response Plan Training Slides." Environmental Protection Agency. Accessed 15 September 2014. http://www.epa.gov/watersecurity/tools/ trainingcd/trainers/NRP.pdf.

———. 2014b. "Office of Cybersecurity and Communications." 9 April. Accessed 3 September 2014. http://www.dhs.gov/office-cybersecurity-and-communications.

———. 2014c. *About the National Cybersecurity and Communications Integration Center*. 15 August. Accessed 3 September 2014. http://www.dhs.gov/about-national-cybersecurity-communications-integration-center.

U.S. Department of Justice. 2007. "Protect America Act of 2007." *Preserving Life and Liberty*. 5 August. Accessed 10 September 2014. http://www.justice.gov/archive/ ll/docs/text-of-paa.pdf.

———. 2009. "Alleged International Hacker Indicted for Massive Attack on U.S. Retail and Banking Networks." *Justice News*. 17 August. Accessed 29 September 2014. http://www.justice.gov/opa/pr/alleged-international-hacker-indicted-massive-attack-us-retail-and-banking-networks.

―――. 2013. "Five Indicted in New Jersey for Largest Known Data Breach Conspiracy." *Justice News*. 25 July. Accessed 29 September 2014. http://www.justice.gov/opa/pr/five-indicted-new-jersey-largest-known-data-breach-conspiracy.

―――. 2014. "Highlights of the USA PATRIOT Act." Accessed 10 September 2014. http://www.justice.gov/archive/ll/highlights.htm.

U.S. Department of the Air Force. 2011. Annex 3-12 *Cyberspace Operations*. 30 November. Accessed 28 May 2014. https://doctrine.af.mil/DTM/dtmcyberspaceops.htm.

―――. 2012. "Cyber Vision 2025: United States Air Force Cyberspace Science and Technology Vision 2012-2025." *Defense Innovation Marketplace*. 13 December. Accessed 9 September 2014. http://www.defenseinnovationmarketplace.mil/resources/cyber/cybervision2025.pdf.

U.S. District Court for the Northern District of California. 2006. *Classified Declaration of John D. Negroponte, Director of National Intelligence* (redacted and declassified version). 12 May. Accessed 1 November 2014. http://www.dni.gov/files/documents/0505/DNI%20Negroponte%202006%20Declassified%20Hepting%20Declaration.pdf.

―――. 2011. "51 Order GRANTING Plaintiff's Motion for a Temporary Restraining Order." *Scribd*. 26 January. Accessed 27 September 2014. http://www.scribd.com/doc/47676628/51-Order-GRANTING-Plaintiff-s-Motion-For-a-Temporary-Restraining-Order.

U.S. Foreign Intelligence Surveillance Court. 2014a. *In Re Application of the Federal Bureau of Investigation for an Order Requiring the Production of Tangible Things from* (Redacted) *Docket Number: BR*. 3 January. Accessed 31 October 2014. http://www.odni.gov/files/documents/BR%2014-01%20Redacted%20Primary%20Order%20(Final).pdf.

―――. 2014b. *About the Foreign Intelligence Surveillance Court*. Accessed 20 May 2014. http://www.fisc.uscourts.gov/about-foreign-intelligence-surveillance-court.

―――. 2014c. *United States Foreign Intelligence Surveillance Court*. Accessed 20 May 2014. http://www.fisc.uscourts.gov/.

U.S. Government. 1959. *National Security Agency Act of 1959*. May. Accessed 10 September 2014. http://www.intelligence.senate.gov/nsaact1959.htm.

―――. 1978. Public Law 95-511–*Electronic Surveillance within the United States for Foreign Intelligence Purposes*. 25 October. Accessed 10 September 2014. http://legislink.org/us/pl-95-511.

————. 2011. Title 50–*War and National Defense*. Accessed 10 September 2014. http://www.gpo.gov/fdsys/pkg/USCODE-2011-title50/pdf/USCODE-2011-title50.pdf.

————. 2012. Title 32–*National Guard*. Accessed 10 September 2014. http://www.gpo.gov/fdsys/pkg/USCODE-2012-title32/pdf/USCODE-2012-title32.pdf.

————. 2013a. Title 6–*Domestic Security*. Accessed 10 September 2014. http://www.gpo.gov/fdsys/pkg/USCODE-2013-title6/pdf/USCODE-2013-title6.pdf.

————. 2013b. Title 10–*Armed Forces*. Accessed 10 September 2014. http://www.gpo.gov/fdsys/pkg/USCODE-2013-title10/pdf/USCODE-2013-title10.pdf.

————. 2013c. Title 18–*Crimes and Criminal Procedure*. Accessed 10 September 2014. http://www.gpo.gov/fdsys/pkg/USCODE-2013-title18/pdf/USCODE-2013-title18-front.pdf.

————. 2014a. U.S. Code: Title 50–*War and National Defense*. Accessed 10 September 2014. http://www.law.cornell.edu/uscode/text/50.

————. 2014b. 50 U.S. Code § 1802-*Electronic surveillance authorization without court order*. Accessed 10 September 2014. http://www.law.cornell.edu/uscode/text/50/1802.

————. 2014c. 50 U.S. Code § 1806 - *Use of information*. Accessed 10 September 2014. http://www.law.cornell.edu/uscode/text/50/1806.

————. 2014d. 50 U.S. Code § 3601 - *Short title*. Accessed 10 September 2014. http://www.law.cornell.edu/uscode/text/50/3601.

U.S. House of Representatives. 2014. "H.R. 3361-USA FREEDOM Act" *113th Congress*. 30 July. Accessed 23 September 2014. https://beta.congress.gov/bill/113th-congress/house-bill/3361/related-bills.

U.S. House of Representatives Permanent Select Committee on Intelligence. 2013. "Intel Committee Chairs and Ranking Members Slated to Meet with President Obama Today on FISA." *Press Releases*. 1 August. Accessed 23 September 2014. http://intelligence.house.gov/press-release/intel-committee-chairs-and-ranking-members-slated-meet-president-obama-today-fisa.

U.S. Legislature. 2014. H.B. 161 *Prohibition on Electronic Data Collection Assistance* (Roberts, M.). 13 March. Accessed 23 September 2014. http://le.utah.gov/~2014/status/hbillsta/hb0161.htm.

U.S. Office of the Director of National Intelligence. 2014. *Newly Declassified Documents Regarding the Now-Discontinued NSA Bulk Electronic Communications Metadata Pursuant To Section 402 of the Foreign Intelligence Surveillance Act.* 11 August. Accessed 1 November 2014. http://icontherecord.tumblr.com/search/declassified.

U.S. President. 1981. Executive Order 12333--*United States Intelligence Activities.* 4 December. Accessed 7 September 2014. http://www.archives.gov/federal-register/codification/executive-order/12333.html.

———. 2003a. "Homeland Security Presidential Directive / HSPD-8." 17 December. Accessed 15 September 2014. http://fas.org/irp/offdocs/nspd/hspd-8.html.

———. 2003b. "Homeland Security Presidential Directive 7: Critical Infrastructure Identification, Prioritization, and Protection." 17 December. Accessed 19 September 2014. http://www.dhs.gov/homeland-security-presidential-directive-7#1.

———. 2003c. "Homeland Security Presidential Directive/HSPD-5." 28 February. Accessed 15 September 2014. http://fas.org/irp/offdocs/nspd/hspd-5.html.

———. 2003d. "The National Strategy to Secure Cyberspace." February. Accessed 24 March 2014. http://georgewbush-whitehouse.archives.gov/pcipb/.

———. 2008a. "National Security Presidential Directive/NSPD-54, Homeland Security Presidential Directive/HSPD-23 (Redacted copy)." 9 January. Accessed 17 September 2014. http://fas.org/irp/offdocs/nspd/nspd-54.pdf.

———. 2008b. Executive Order 12333 *United States Intelligence Activities (As amended by Executive Orders 13284 (2003), 13355 (2004) and 13470 (2008)).* 31 July. Accessed 12 November 2014. http://georgewbush-whitehouse.archives.gov/news/releases/2008/07/20080731-2.html.

———. 2009a. "The Comprehensive National Cybersecurity Initiative." Accessed 19 March 2014. http://www.whitehouse.gov/issues/foreign-policy/cybersecurity/national-initiative.

———. 2009b. Presidential Policy Directive - 1: *Organization of the National Security Council System.* 13 February. Accessed 15 September 2014. https://www.hsdl.org/?view&did=34560.

———. 2010. *National Security Strategy.* May. Accessed 28 May 2014. http://www.whitehouse.gov/sites/default/files/rss_viewer/national_security_strategy.pdf.

———. 2011a. *International Strategy for Cyberspace: Prosperity, Security and Openness in a Networked World.* May. Accessed 20 September 2014. http://www.whitehouse.gov/sites/default/files/rss_viewer/international_strategy_for_cyberspace.pdf.

———. 2011b. *National Strategy for Counterterrorism.* June. Accessed 20 September 2014. http://www.whitehouse.gov/sites/default/files/counterterrorism_strategy.pdf.

———. 2011c. *Strategy to Combat Transnational Organized Crime.* July. Accessed 20 September 2014. http://www.whitehouse.gov/sites/default/files/Strategy_to_Combat_Transnational_Organized_Crime_July_2011.pdf.

———. 2012. Executive Order - *Establishing the White House Homeland Security Partnership Council.* 26 October. Accessed 20 September 2014. http://www.whitehouse.gov/the-press-office/2012/10/26/executive-order-establishing-white-house-homeland-security-partnership-c.

———. 2013a. Executive Order -- *Improving Critical Infrastructure Cybersecurity.* 12 February. Accessed 20 September 2014. http://www.whitehouse.gov/the-press-office/2013/02/12/executive-order-improving-critical-infrastructure-cybersecurity.

———. 2013b. Executive Order 13636 - *Improving Critical Infrastructure Cybersecurity.* 19 February. Accessed 15 September 2014. http://www.gpo.gov/fdsys/pkg/FR-2013-02-19/pdf/2013-03915.pdf.

———. 2013c. Presidential Policy Directive 21 -- *Critical Infrastructure Security and Resilience.* 12 February. Accessed 19 September 2014. http://www.whitehouse.gov/the-press-office/2013/02/12/presidential-policy-directive-critical-infrastructure-security-and-resil.

———. 2014. Presidential Policy Directive 28 -- *Signals Intelligence Activities.* 17 January. Accessed 19 September 2014. http://www.whitehouse.gov/the-press-office/2014/01/17/presidential-policy-directive-signals-intelligence-activities.

U.S. Secretary of Defense. 2012. *Sustaining U.S. Global Leadership: Priorities for 21st Century Defense.* 5 January. Accessed 21 September 2014. http://www.defense.gov/news/defense_strategic_guidance.pdf.

———. 2013. *Strategy for Homeland Defense and Defense Support of Civil Authorities.* February. Accessed 20 September 2014. http://www.defense.gov/news/homelanddefensestrategy.pdf.

———. 2014. *Quadrennial Defense Review.* 4 March. Accessed 28 May 2014. http://www.defense.gov/pubs/2014_Quadrennial_Defense_Review.pdf.

U.S. Secretary of Homeland Security. 2012. *Department of Homeland Security Strategic Plan: Fiscal Years 2012-2016.* 13 February. Accessed 29 May 2014. http://www.dhs.gov/xlibrary/assets/dhs-strategic-plan-fy-2012-2016.pdf.

U.S. Secret Service. 2013. *U.S. Secret Service Annual Report.* Accessed 3 September 2014. http://www.secretservice.gov/USSS_FY13AR.pdf.

———. 2014a. *Secret Service History.* Accessed 3 September 2014. http://www.secretservice.gov/history.shtml.

———. 2014b. *United States Secret Service Strategic Plan 2014-2018.* Accessed 16 August 2014. http://www.secretservice.gov/usss_strategic_plan_2014_2018.pdf.

U.S. Senate Committee on Commerce, Science, and Transportation. 2013. *A "Kill Chain" Analysis of the 2013 Target Data Breach.* 26 March. Accessed 10 September 2014. http://www.commerce.senate.gov/public/?a=Files. Serve&File_id=24d3c229-4f2f-405d-b8db-a3a67f183883.

U.S. Strategic Command, Public Affairs Office. 2014. "Command Snapshot." *U.S. Strategic Command Snapshot.* Accessed 9 September 2014. http://www.stratcom.mil/snapshot/

Value Walk Staff. 2014."California Assembly Panel Votes to Turn off NSA Water." *Value Walk.* 24 June. Accessed 23 September 2014. http://www.valuewalk.com/ 2014/06/nsa-water-turned-off/.

Van Voris, Bob. 2014. "Microsoft Fails to Block U.S. Warrant for Ireland E-Mail." *Bloomberg.* 31 July. Accessed 30 September 2014. http://www.bloomberg.com/ news/2014-07-31/microsoft-fails-to-block-u-s-warrant-for-ireland-e-mail.html.

Veracode. 2011. "Possible PlayStation Network Attack Vectors." *Veracode.* 13 May. Accessed 28 September 2014. https://www.veracode.com/blog/2011/05/possible-playstation-network-attack-vectors.

Villeneuve, Nart. 2014. "Where have all the credit cards gone? The Cybercrime Underground and Its Ties to Eastern Europe." *FireEye Blog.* 3 February. Accessed 24 September 2014. http://www.fireeye.com/blog/corporate/2014/02/ where-have-all-the-credit-cards-gone-the-cybercrime-underground-and-its-ties-to-eastern-europe.html.

The Washington Post. 2013. *NSA Secrets: Government Spying in the Internet Age.* New York, NY: Diversion Books, 2013. 17 December. http://www.amazon.com/NSA-Secrets-Government-Spying-Internet-ebook/dp/B00HEQZMWE/ref=sr_ 1_1?ie=UTF8&qid=1414564100&sr=8-1&keywords=NSA+Secrets%3A+ Government+Spying+in+the+Internet+Age.

Webster, Andrew. 2011. "FBI Investigating PSN Hack; Sony Looking Into Compensating Users." *Ars Technica.* 29 April. Accessed 28 September 2014. http://arstechnica.com/gaming/2011/04/sony-looking-into-compensating-psn-users-fbi-gets-involved/.

Westervelt, Robert. 2014. "Sony Agrees To $15 Million Payout, Free PS3 Games In PlayStation Breach Settlement." *CRN: News, Analysis, and Perspective for Vars and Technology Integrators.* 17 June. Accessed 27 September 2014. http://www.crn.com/news/security/300073160/sony-agrees-to-15-million-payout-free-ps3-games-in-playstation-breach-settlement.htm.

The White House. 2014. "Remarks by Secretary of Homeland Security Jeh Johnson at The White House Cybersecurity Framework Event." *News.* 12 February. Accessed 28 May 2014. http://www.dhs.gov/news/2014/02/12/remarks-secretary-homeland-security-jeh-johnson-white-house-cybersecurity-framework.

White House Press Secretary. 2013. "Fact Sheet: Presidential Policy Directive on Critical Infrastructure Security and Resilience." Statements & Releases. 12 February. Accessed 19 September 2014. http://www.whitehouse.gov/the-press-office/2013/02/12/fact-sheet-presidential-policy-directive-critical-infrastructure-securit.

———. 2014. "Remarks by the President on Review of Signals Intelligence." 17 January. Accessed September 23, 2014. http://www.whitehouse.gov/the-press-office/2014/01/17/remarks-president-review-signals-intelligence.

Whittaker, Azck. 2013. "Obama's Cybersecurity Executive Order: What You Need to Know." *ZDNet.* 13 February. Accessed 20 September 2014. http://www.zdnet.com/obamas-cybersecurity-executive-order-what-you-need-to-know-7000011221/.

www.ingramcontent.com/pod-product-compliance
Lightning Source LLC
Chambersburg PA
CBHW081215280526
45787CB00006B/2418